Absolute Vision

What if the life we imagined isn't the one we have been living? What does it take to make impossible dreams come true, especially when it feels easier to give up? Absolute Vision is an engaging, insightful collaboration by twenty-one men and women from Canada, the United States of America, South Africa, the United Kingdom, Nicaragua and Bulgaria. The authors have teamed up to share their motivational, personal, TRUE STORIES of achieving their vision and intentionally creating an extraordinary life against all odds.

Whether you believe in a higher power, rely on your own sheer determination, or question your beliefs and your purpose, you're sure to find inspiration within these pages.

A collaboration by **Jo Pronger Faulkner**

Co-authored by

Roxane Archer, Patti Bevilacqua, Mike Boone, Christina Carlos, Kathy A. Davis, Karlo Dominguez, Kristina L. Foster, Mimi Hricko, Beverly Jacobson, Lindsay Malkinson, Sonia Aldana Morales, Tanya Newbould, Daniela Panetta, Nathan Pendleton, Jennifer D. Scharf, Rosa Lopez Silva, Shari Hall Smith, Greta Trefalt, Petar Valkanov, Deborah Vick

Foreword by **Caitlin Alifirenka**

Absolute Vision

Print ISBN: 978-1-7775628-4-7

Table of Contents

Acknowledgments

To the men and women in this collaboration: each of you should be incredibly proud of such an accomplishment as this. I am proud of you. I am inspired by you. And I am grateful to have you in this book, sharing your story and putting yourself out there as vulnerably as each of you have. Whether you were already a published author before this book or not, I know writing your chapter wasn't easy. Thank you from the bottom of my heart for giving this your all.

Thank you to our beta readers: Shari Hall Smith, Doreen Stroud, Rachel Kuehn, Anne Neville, my mother-in-law Mar Boone, and my lifelong friends, Jennifer Winter, and Heather Roy. Your thoroughness, attention to detail, and the helpful feedback from each of you made this publication the best it could possibly be.

Thank you, C.B. Moore, for your expert editing skills, your understanding, and your humor. Twenty-one different writing styles in one book pose some unique challenges, and, as always, you've been a joy to work with.

Thank you, Kristina L. Foster, for designing such a stunning book cover that pairs perfectly with the first collaboration in this series, *Absolute Will*. Symbolizing transformation between conscious and unconscious, and our thoughts versus our feelings and intuition, wooden docks also represent strength, stability, and going through tough emotions — things every story here touches on. It's so fitting that we can't quite see what's in the distance, just like most journeys into the unknown as we chase our dreams and visions.

Special thanks to Shari Hall Smith for offering to lead our public relations strategy, write our press release, and contact key people who you knew would want to hear more about this book, our stories, and our mission. I love your heart, I value your true collaborative spirit, and I am so grateful for you.

To my husband, Mike: I'm so proud of you for dreaming big, staying forever hopeful, and doing whatever it takes to make your vision happen, against all odds. Thank you for never giving up on me, for believing in me, and not only embracing most of my crazy ideas along the way but also bringing a bunch of your own to the party. I am grateful for our growth together as we've worked hard to build our dream in Nicaragua while re-building our life in Canada, and I'm inspired by your dedication to the life-changing project for which this collaboration is fundraising. Thank you for writing your chapter in this book, despite the emotional journey you found yourself on in the process. I'm excited to be on this ride with you!

And finally, thank you, Caitlin Alifirenka, for your praise of these stories. I am excited to have connected with you through your wonderful mom, Anne Neville, whom Mike and I are blessed to have in our circle. I've known for a good long while now that there was something special about your book, even though it took me years to start flipping through the pages. The moment I did just that, I realized I needed to ask if you would write our foreword. It's absolutely perfect.

~ *Jo Pronger Faulkner*

Foreword

*A*bsolute Vision* is must-read for those who want to find a way to achieve and succeed!

As a teenager, I helped my former pen pal, Martin Ganda, achieve his dreams of coming to the United States to study. It was challenging and taught me monumental obstacles CAN be moved and rearranged.

Jo Pronger Faulkner proves over and over again, through her story and those of the other authors, that determination and a positive vision empowers one to succeed. Like me, these optimistic authors set clear, attainable goals.

I embraced my abilities as a teenager and gained confidence through small, yet effective steps. My support system (family) kept me focusing on my clear vision of what I needed to do and how to do it.

Because of their positive statements and guidance, I achieved my own goals...having my pen pal arrive in the USA! Watching Martin walk through the entry gate onto United States soil, I proved to myself that the wisdom and tenacity of a young adult is powerful with a clear, absolute vision.

~ *Caitlin Alifirenka, co-author of the New York Times and International Best Selling YA dual memoir, I Will Always Write Back: How One Letter Changed Two Lives.*

CHAPTER 1

Roller Coasters and Teeter-Totters

Jo Pronger Faulkner

I 'd been racking my brain for months over what kind of fundraiser could bring in the amount of money we would need. This wasn't something a friendly neighborhood poker tournament or cupcake sale would cover. This was big. It was going to take some serious coin to do it. Not only that, but fundraising donors also usually expect an incentive for their donation. I was having trouble coming up with any decent idea that would get donors excited.

Sitting at the small wooden table that doubled as a computer desk and room divider between our kitchen and living room, I looked up from my laptop at the vision board across the room. Pictures and words were scattered across the oversized cork board that took up a three-foot-by-three section on the wall. The first few vision boards my then-fiancé Mike and I had created over the years had been much smaller, usually just using cardstock paper, but on December 31, 2020, we really upped our game building this one. I know just enough about Feng Shui to know it works, and to make sure we attracted the right energy flow to the wall representing inspiration, reputation, and career, we needed to add something red. Mike — a rustic furniture hobbyist — happened to have a red-painted shipping pallet, so he had ripped it apart to use the boards as a frame for our vision board, making a big, bold statement in the room.

My eyes landed on one picture in particular: a cute, small, one-level house with a big, covered, wraparound porch. When I searched online for "Caribbean houses" and found the photo, it seemed perfect, so I had printed it out and pinned it to the cork.

My gaze shifted in the opposite direction to look out the window and I let my mind wander. I started to think about what that little Caribbean house would be like in real life, not just in a picture. What would the layout be like inside and what would it feel like to walk through the rooms? What would the wall colors be? What delicious aromas would fill the kitchen at mealtimes?

I imagined every detail, though it wasn't real yet. It was a house I had never been in, yet I was so invested in visualizing it I could see and smell every detail. I could hear the breeze rustling the wide, flat leaves of the plantain and banana trees in the yard where this little imaginary house nestled.

A wave of goosebumps came over me and tears began to well up in my eyes. My face felt tingly. This was ginormous — gigantic and enormous — as well as joyous and fulfilling all at once. I was really in the moment, not just seeing the vision but experiencing it too. I took my time and let myself feel what it would be like when the project was finally done, everything finished and in its proper place. Though we hadn't even begun yet, I imagined the family's excitement as we handed them their new keys.

One of the tears escaped from the corner of my eye and trickled down my cheek. My throat tightened up. I felt overwhelmed in the best way possible.

It's one thing to build a house for yourself. But it's a very different story to build one for someone else.

The five years leading up to this project were like riding on several twisty emotional and financial roller coasters going in different directions. It was as though the universe would say, "Here, hold my beer" whenever we decided the last thing we had just been through was probably the worst of it.

Our ups and downs had been monumental. Mike and I had both been dealing with stressful, expensive divorces, numerous court dates and mountains of paperwork. I had battled four autoimmune diseases that made me so sick I wasn't able to save my 15-year government career, and then I was also diagnosed with invasive melanoma (skin cancer) and needed surgery.

After finalizing my divorce, Mike and I went to Nicaragua for a vacation, fell in love with a remote Caribbean island called Big Corn Island, excitedly bought two acres of jungle land, and started building a two-suite vacation house that was to be the first of several. We endured setbacks during construction and many more costs than we had naively budgeted, and in the middle of that project we came back to Canada penniless, with only two suitcases and nowhere to call home. We had sunk everything into our Caribbean property, thinking that once it was built we would start renting it out and make our money back. Except we couldn't afford to finish it. And then, after almost giving up on everything, including myself, I was able to turn my health around through diet and lifestyle changes and started earning an income again. I got my life back.

Our financial situation recovered relatively quickly in Canada. But two disastrous experiences with expat house-sitters we had arranged for our Nicaragua property drove me to my wit's end. I was ready to throw in the towel and wave goodbye to our Caribbean dream. However, we couldn't sell it the way it was, still unfinished. We had too much invested in it, and at that point we would never have gotten back the money we had put in.

At the very least, we needed to get it finished, so we decided to be more intentional about surrounding ourselves with reliable, trustworthy people. After careful consideration, we offered a hard-working, well-respected local family to move in and look after the house and our dogs. We had known them for a couple of years, and they had a solid reputation in the community.

As it turned out, the family had been on the verge of homelessness. They, too, had experienced monumental ups and downs, and the timing couldn't have been more perfect for all of us.

The longer they house-sat and helped us finish our vacation home, the more we got to know them, and know their incredible story of resilience. Most Nicaraguan people live in poverty. A typical laborer's wage on Big Corn Island is only US$10 per day, making it nearly impossible to pay for necessities, let alone save anything extra. Eventually, Mike and I decided that we really wanted to build this family a house of their own. But while

8

we weren't in dire straits anymore, we also weren't exactly rolling in extra cash, and we hadn't figured out what the next steps could be.

In mid-2020 I started writing a book about my success in reversing the autoimmune diseases I'd had, which turned out to be an emotional journey of its own. During the five months it took to write it, I connected with many other people who had similar stories to mine: they had overcome significant health crises, had persevered, and gone on to lead fulfilling lives. I started to wonder if a collection of inspirational stories might be a worthwhile publishing project but immediately felt dread in the pit of my stomach.

I had managed large groups of people in my government career, and had managed all kinds of projects, but the minute I started thinking about stepping out of my comfort zone to create a book collaboration, my inner critic put me back in my place.

I'm not qualified to run a book collaboration; I've got no credibility as an author yet, let alone as a writing coach and a publisher for other people. Self-publishing is a huge undertaking of time and there are costs too. How would that work? Would the authors pay? Is this just done as a volunteer project? Who would want to do this with me if I don't even know how it all works? Who am I kidding?

In early 2021, soon after I published my autoimmune healing story, someone I knew announced she was doing a book collaboration and I felt torn. *This could be me. This is what I want to do. And I've got experience now publishing my first book. So why am I not doing it?* I went back and forth in a state of double "FOMO" — a fear of missing out. I was missing out on the opportunity to be running my own collaboration yet felt like I still wasn't ready for some reason, and I didn't want to miss out on this while struggling to get to the bottom of my procrastination.

I continued to let my back-and-forth thoughts run amok and jumped into my friend's book instead. It was her first collaboration; each author paid to be in it. Watching her navigate the process as we collectively rolled along, I was reminded we often learn more effectively by doing, and my experience writing and publishing my own book meant I knew more than I'd given myself credit for.

I have spent a lifetime working on my confidence, yet there was fear, staring me in the face. My self-talk kept preventing me from taking action. It wasn't that I didn't know how to lead a group or publish a book; I was worried about being looked to for writing guidance and not delivering, and was scared of screwing it up for people who would be blindly trusting my imposturous leadership. When you publish a book, you get one shot at it, and then it's out there for the world to read and judge. On the flip side, my intuition was excitedly screaming at me that the type of collaboration I was considering had the potential to be spectacular, and that made me nervous, too.

Sometimes it feels easier to wait; time will eventually make our decision for us one way or another, and waiting takes the onus off us as the responsible party if things go wrong. But the opportunity cost of procrastination can be just as debilitating as aiming high and missing the target. We get stuck on a teeter-totter of *should I or shouldn't I* until it's too late.

Sitting at my table, gazing out the window, my mind swirling with thoughts of books, the power of personal stories, and the family's house we would someday build, the idea suddenly became so obvious I couldn't believe I hadn't thought of it before: a book collaboration was a perfect way to fundraise!

My fear seemed to evaporate into thin air as a fire was lit in my heart. We were about to make a family's homeownership dreams come true, and what a unique way to give back to the fundraising donors: they would get to become published authors and experience the joy that comes from playing a direct role in helping other people in a life-changing way. Finally, I was more excited than scared, and it gave me an energy about collaborating I hadn't felt before.

I came up with criteria for the types of stories I would be looking for, and I announced I was accepting author applications for the book I titled *Absolute Will*. As each author joined the project over the next few months, I became more emotional about the caliber of people this project was attracting, and more comfortable in my ability to lead day by day, one step at a time. When I saw the first rough drafts of the chapters, many of the stories brought me to tears, and I knew this was going to be an incredible book.

By mid-October 2021, after hundreds of hours spent at my computer, it was a real, published book with twenty-one women from seven countries around the world, each sharing inspirational stories of willpower when facing a health crisis. It became an international best-seller within a matter of weeks, hitting #1 best seller in nine categories across three countries, and #1 new release in 31 categories across four countries. For many of the authors this was their first-ever writing endeavor. What a way to debut.

The money raised from the author's chapter entries and subsequent sales of the book helped me and Mike finally start seeing "the home collaborations built" come to life, brick by brick. We were on Big Corn Island to start building in early January 2022; the family's youngest daughter helped Mike stake out the foundation's footprint, all the family members excitedly helped along the way, and we got the house to lock-up in a few short months — the concrete foundation was poured, the walls and roof were built, and the doors and windows were installed — but it wasn't livable yet.

After we came back to Canada, a local island construction crew continued building throughout 2022 using funds from additional donors and author entry fees from the new collaboration I embarked on, *Absolute Vision*. Interestingly, despite starting the house build from a design Mike had in his head, after several changes during early construction days the real house looks almost exactly like the picture we had on our vision board. It's funny how that happens.

When it comes to achieving our vision, fighting *for* or *against* something is motivation's secret weapon: the more intensely we feel about what we want or don't want, the stronger our focus will be to take action. In creating *Absolute Will*, I actually experienced both. My fear turned into excitement when I realized a book collaboration would be an impactful fundraiser; my motivation was that the house we wanted to build would change a family's life forever. I was *fighting for them.*

What I also often find myself *fighting against* is regret. I don't want to forever be left wondering what might have been or wishing I had "given it a good go," and no one else is going to do it for me. I have purposely used this as a decision-making tool many times in my life to talk myself into all kinds of outside-my-comfort-zone things that became my most favorite adventures and epic experiences. If I'll regret *not* doing something, I know it means I'm going to need to figure out a way to do it. While sometimes we get stuck going back and forth when facing a decision, paradoxically that teeter-totter effect can actually be a useful motivator if it doubles up our sense of urgency to take action.

The minute my mind merged my two ideas into one, it was as though the stars aligned. When I considered charging authors to be in a book collaboration but had never run one before, it felt inauthentic to run it as a credible business. I felt uneasy, and fear became my excuse. But a book collaboration as a fundraiser felt absolutely perfect. Building a home for a family in need was so much more important than worrying about how it would all work, and the life-changing impact for them became my reason to do it. I felt energized, ready to make it happen no matter what it took, and I was suddenly all-in. Finding my deeper "why" to do the collaboration changed my perspective and increased the intensity level of my motivation.

Having an excited vibe about what you're doing, and taking action to get going, attracts more positive energy and builds momentum too. Not only was the collaboration successful, allowing us to start building the family's house, but through one of the authors I also discovered a new remote-work opportunity that checked all the boxes of a career for me. The company's motto is "no family left behind," our team's unique culture is all about each of us achieving our dreams by helping other people achieve theirs, and I can't help but notice the vision of the company and team fits so well with mine. I feel as though everything came together at the right time, for the right reasons, with the right people.

Was *Absolute Will* more work than I had anticipated? Yes. Did I have days where I wasn't as excited? Of course. If you ask me those questions about the subsequent house construction project, I'll answer yes to those too. But I truly believe our most meaningful personal growth happens in the process of doing seemingly impossible things. There's a special type of self-assurance that comes from taking personal responsibility, tapping into our willpower, persevering despite the discomfort, and successfully getting through the tough stuff, time after time — the type of self-assurance that isn't possible to acquire any other way.

I also believe we become better versions of ourselves through helping others in impactful ways. Bringing authors together to collectively share their stories with the world and building a house for a family that didn't have one are experiences that have changed me forever.

Life is full of roller coasters and teeter-totters, and going after big dreams can feel impossible some days. An extraordinary result, and an extraordinary life, don't happen all by themselves. When you decide what you truly want, focus on your vision, get excited, experience every detail with all your senses, and take consistent action in going after it, you'll be unstoppable.

About the Author

Jo Pronger Faulkner is an international best-selling author, business owner, collaboration creator, holistic lifestyle coach (nutrition/ health/ finances/ collaborations), animal lover, and nature enthusiast living in northwestern Ontario, Canada with her husband Mike and their rescue dog Jemison. Jo's last name is now Boone since she and Mike were married in the summer of 2022, and she continues to publish books using her maiden name, Faulkner.

Jo and Mike are both Pisces, plant-based foodies, adventure-seekers, and they are obsessed with renovation projects, vision boards, and building their Caribbean jungle retreat, *Drifter's Claim*.

Jo has a Bachelor of Commerce degree from Royal Roads University in Victoria, British Columbia, and multiple provincial Life and A&S (accident and sickness) insurance licenses across Canada. She has certificates in body healing, aromatherapy, nutrition coaching, financial management, and equine science. Her unique background includes working in social services, finance, insurance/investments/wealth management, human resources, real estate, animal health, and with small business start-ups. She has also volunteered with a children's adoption organization, several animal health/rescue organizations, and, along with Mike, as fundraising and project managers of "the home collaborations built."

Jo's first book, *The Autoimmune Warrior's Healing Key*, is a motivational #1 best-selling book about her struggle with autoimmune illness, how the endocrine system works, and her discovery of the healing power of plants. She was a co-author in the #1 best-seller *The Truth About Success,* co-author/creator of the #1 international best-seller *Absolute Will,* and creator of this collaboration, *Absolute Vision.*

Through sharing her personal story in books, podcasts, interviews, across social media, and in her autoimmune healing group, Jo is inspiring autoimmune warriors around the world to listen to their intuition, understand their core values, and to start making intentional choices to live the "high-vibing" life they truly desire.

You can connect with Jo here:

Websites:
https://joprongerboone.com/
https://boondockspublishing.com/

Linktree:
https://linktr.ee/JoProngerFaulkner (social media links)

CHAPTER 2

The Gift

Shari Hall Smith

"W"hy did you tell me that?" I asked, chewing the inside of my mouth. My palms had become noticeably sweaty, and my right knee began to twitch.

"Well, because most people want to know," the woman replied from the other side of the desk.

I took a deep breath and leaned in, placing my elbows on her desk. Taking my time to choose words that would be impactful rather than emotional, and yet wanting to make an obvious point, I looked steadily into her eyes.

"You should really wait until someone asks you the question before assuming. And what kind of prediction is one to five years, anyway? It's a pretty big range to be throwing around, don't you think? Especially when you do not know me."

My greatest fear is fear. And my way of dealing with it is to act tough and aggressive while inside I am weak and terrified, a complete people-pleasing weenie. The aftermath of confrontation leaves me sweating when no one else would have ever guessed it.

Walking back out through the double doors of the building, I shook my head and arms, trying to wake myself from what had to be a bad dream.

I cannot believe this is happening to me. Again.

My first breast cancer diagnosis came at age thirty-six. I had just become engaged; I was planning a life of happiness and the joy of a family. Listening to the doctor sharing the news over the phone, I had silently given a thumbs down to my sister Debbie and my fiancé Greg and then stared past them, emotionless. Calling my parents, who were awaiting the results, brought outbursts of emotion from them I can never forget.

That night as I lay in bed, in my mind I went through the entire process of the pain I was about to cause my loved ones. I feared my own suffering and eventual excruciating death as my thoughts focused on Mary Jo, my dear friend who had died four years earlier at just thirty-seven years old, leaving a husband and two young children behind. She was my reason for getting the lump checked in the first place after I discovered it. If not for the devastating loss of her, I am certain I would have missed the lump or ignored it. Mary Jo very well may have saved my life.

As the sun rose the next morning, I vowed to never again make a bad thing worse by letting those negative thoughts take over. When those thoughts inevitably crept up, I would remember how horrific that sleepless night was.

My medical team had advised my treatment should consist of surgery, six months of chemotherapy and five years of tamoxifen. I sought a few more opinions and became further confused. The chemo would compromise my immune system and cause possible health issues later, and the tamoxifen would put me into menopause, which would severely lessen any chances of having children. As I drove home one day, following one of those nerve-racking consults, my fear consumed me — and while making a left turn, I barely escaped causing a head-on collision. I pulled over and parked at the side of the road, gripping the wheel, my chest ready to explode as I hyperventilated, when I figured it out: *There are no guarantees, and I could have been taken from this earth just now.*

I decided to choose my best quality of life. I would do the surgery with no adjunctive therapy, and I was hopeful this strategy would allow me to have children.

This was before the internet, before pink ribbons, and before the sisterhood that now has opened a world of conversations and support. Because Mary Jo gifted me with early detection, the surgery was a success, and I became compelled to spread awareness that early detection is vital and provides time to explore additional options.

Greg's advertising agency enabled me to produce professional television commercials sharing my personal story. My goal was to inspire others and to encourage women to be their own health advocate, rather than fearing the diagnosis. I was one of the early members of The National Breast Cancer Coalition, which embarked on a grassroots effort around the country to collect signatures requesting research funding for breast cancer and present the request to then-President Clinton. I was honored to be invited to the White House for the bill signing in October 1993, and it remains in the top tier of prideful, productive moments in my life to have been part of this historic event and to have shaken President Clinton's hand.

After the bill signing and meet and greet, I was interviewed for my local television station to air the event. I can still recall that news clip and the words I spoke. I looked healthy and felt excited to have experienced this worthwhile project, and I said, "If I have daughters someday, my hope is they never have to deal with breast cancer." As part of the event, we all went to the National Museum of Women in D.C. to view The Faces of Breast Cancer, a life-sized photo exhibit illustrating extraordinary women and their journey with breast cancer. My smile had shifted into dismay as I realized all of them had died from the disease, and it suddenly changed my high "I can do anything" mood into Why. Not. Me. Too.

I was in a dipper of a mood as I boarded the plane from D.C. back to Rochester, New York, and I felt foolish over the delusion that I would survive this disease.

Mary Jo's passing inspired me to make a change in as many outcomes as possible, sharing acceptance, engaging in conversations to support what was historically private or embarrassing, and to acknowledge that many live after this diagnosis. I needed to relieve my own fear and place my focus on healing; it was no longer a choice. I was compelled to create something that could inspire hope and illustrate just how vital early detection is. I decided to create a photo exhibit featuring those who lived with their inspiring stories, and named it Faces of Hope. It would feature women and men, representing a variety of races and ages, delivering valuable — and ideally, life-saving — impact for everyone who saw it.

My vision, along with Greg's advertising agency and connections, would bring Faces of Hope exhibits to various regions and reach many people with the vital message of early detection in the next decade. The effort grew into a non-profit charity with golf tournaments and business sponsors, as well as developing the first website to connect those who had been diagnosed to others online around the world based on personal and medical criteria.

This project was so near and dear to my heart that even on our wedding day we took time out of our celebrations to film a commercial that Kodak aired around the world in 16 languages. A few months later I was pregnant with our first daughter Sydney, and then blessed a second time with Emma. All my dreams were now my reality.

As time went on, I found that by forging ahead in leading this mission, I could avoid focusing on my own fears — a feat that made my life decidedly easier at the time. But, ironically, putting myself in a position of leadership made me feel like I was navigating this mission alone, and I was never able to join the sisterhood of support that I had nurtured. While happier not dwelling on the negatives, I also felt lonely under the responsibility of holding everyone else up. I came across as strong and capable yet was reliving haunting events in my mind that would be better off relinquished.

The decision to exit from the cancer world was challenging; quitting my volunteer job was more difficult than I imagined. Many of my colleagues attempted to persuade me to partake in their efforts, but I knew it was time to stay home and raise my beloved girls. I cherish the time I have been blessed with them, nurturing a lasting relationship that is loving, honest and supportive. Sydney and Emma have validated my life, and my decision to spend more time with them seemed to make sense to everyone who had been against me after my initial cancer diagnosis, when I decided not to follow medical advice.

So, twenty-two years later when I was diagnosed again, this time stage 4 — metastatic breast cancer to my bones — and informed there was no cure, I was shocked. My daughters had only ever known me after cancer; the first time around, it was early stage, and post-surgery I had focused on being holistic for about a year. Then, when I got pregnant, I ate pizza and crème brûlée every chance I got! Both girls have participated in most of my advocacy efforts and have been veterans to philanthropy since birth.

This time it took longer than one sleepless night to get back on the positivity track. It was terrifying, and my family was devastated. Both my daughters were in severe emotional shock and encountered serious setbacks that took years of time and effort to curtail, or at least minimize. The prognosis keeps the elephant in the room to this day.

For ten weeks I googled cures, and while I did not find one, I did learn about many other treatments and protocols outside what Western medicine offered. I holed up in sweatpants, avoiding humans and showers, searching the internet by day and rewatching 180 episodes of Desperate Housewives by night.

I again refused two of the three treatments advised by my oncologist and found my way to a German cancer clinic for whole body hyperthermia and other immune-building treatments. I traveled to the clinic alone. I had many offers from companions to be with me; however, it was easier for me to negate my fears by being solo — it made it seem not as real. At the clinic, I met incredible people from around the world who had found their way there just like I did, so the bonding was immediate. After our treatments we would sit on the patio and share cancer knowledge.

I cannot stress enough the importance of understanding that no one's cancer journey is the same; not how you got there or how you get out of it. It is vital to understand your own body, mind, and spirit, and I allowed myself the time to feel the understandable distress since this diagnosis was much more dire than the first. My focus remained on retaining a positive mindset, which did finally reappear after making the decision about my treatment plan, and once I was clear on my path, I chose Good Vibes Only as my mantra.

One evening my brother Steve told me he felt I was keeping my fears to myself. He decided to fly to Germany to be with me despite the extensive project he was working on in the US. I kept pushing back, attempting to convince him I was fine, but as soon as I saw him walking towards me at the train station my eyes filled with tears. I was so very grateful for his heart-filled mission. Why do I work so hard to shut off those who want to comfort and support me? I had placed other people ahead of me for a very long time; honoring my self-worth by making myself a priority was a task that still lay years in the future.

Soon after I returned to the US, my scan showed no evidence of disease, which garnered interest and media coverage detailing this unexpected result. People from around the world began to find and connect with me asking for advice. I was dedicated to answering each one individually until one evening, exhausted and trying to write back to seventeen people I had never met, I knew I needed a better plan.

Right then I designed a website that contained all my resources so that when I received an inquiry, I could answer with a website link to read first and then answer any questions after that. This led to people telling me they saw what I did but needed to understand how I did it. How did I choose a different path than what my medical team had advised? How was I not afraid?

I believe we all can make a decision to put fear aside, and I have always maintained it's important to not make a bad thing worse. It has been my choice to not allow circumstances to define me, but rather choose how I deal with them. It was challenging for me to try to teach other people how to develop this mindset, so I thought a physical support may be helpful.

I started making gemstone bracelets with healing meanings and sharing them with those who are struggling. I would say, "When you feel afraid or confused, hold your bracelet and remember that if I can do this, so can you; we all have the power of choosing our outcomes." I began to design different styles inspired by people along my own journey, weaving their stories into the meaning of the gemstone and adding a healing-intention card to accompany the bracelet. The demand began a line of "challenge into empowerment" bracelets, and after considering several business names I kept circling back to one in particular that defined the purpose conclusively. I trademarked and named my company, and since then file my taxes, receive emails addressed to it and say it aloud daily: got ballZ.

Really. As I write this, I still shake my head and chuckle!

These bracelets were added to my website, and the sales proceeds were donated to holistic cancer programs — meaning the outliers who focused on root cause and not symptoms, all non-pharmaceutical. I have utilized both Western and Eastern treatments, but I believe it's important to investigate and understand further how to heal ourselves rather than solely medicate, allowing our bodies to heal as they were intended to do. I have been challenged by many medical practitioners about my integrative path but apparently thirty years later I am still here and sharing my story. I have learned that our minds are powerful, whether we research and rely on our intuition or to choose to live in the present and put fear aside to make better decisions.

I understand now that I received a gift when this all began. I see how challenges can pull off the layers to reveal who we are rather than what happens to us. The gift was discovering that the choice was always mine in terms of how to deal with not just this part of my journey but, in fact, every issue I would encounter going forward.

Hindsight illuminates how inspiration from honoring Mary Jo compelled me to have far-sighted vision: sharing the importance of early detection with others. Empowerment came through facing all the challenges and processing my own fears. It took the second diagnosis and being a support to everyone else for me to develop a more near-sighted view: it was vital to heal myself through recognizing and accepting my self-worth.

About the Author

Shari Hall Smith is an American-born mother, health advocate, and philanthropist with an unused bachelor's degree in Political Science. She is a marketing executive, entrepreneur, social media strategist, and "never take no 'er."

Shari is enjoying producing a charity fundraising event and running an online business after a career in media sales and management in three markets: Rochester, New York; Miami, Florida; and Tampa, Florida.

Diagnosed in her thirties with breast cancer, Shari reframed the priorities in her life including the decision to leave the corporate world to raise her two daughters and start Faces of Hope, a 501(c)(3) charity. She has worked in fundraising with numerous cancer organizations and hospitals, and was one of the grassroots members of the National Breast Cancer Coalition. Shari was named a Woman of Distinction, which was awarded by the New York State Senate, and received the CHAMP award from Cancer Action.

Shari's website offers health advocacy resources and merchandise sales to benefit charities. She is a serial researcher and is passionate about sharing her findings on her website and with anyone who listens. Her quest to heal the root cause of her health issues has spanned over three decades and proven effective against all odds.

Shari has recently moved from upstate New York to Palm Springs, California. She enjoys spending time with loved ones, walking and talking, home design, and advocacy projects. Her greatest life achievement and validation with her husband Greg are their daughters, Sydney and Emma, who work and reside in Los Angeles, California.

Shari has enjoyed writing her story for *Absolute Vision*, which is her first published work.

You can connect with Shari here:

Website:
https://gotballz.org/

Instagram:
https://www.instagram.com/youvegotballz/

LinkedIn:
https://www.linkedin.com/in/shari-hall-smith-5818361a/

CHAPTER 3

Into the Unknown

Kristina L. Foster

I struggled to take deep breaths as the blanket over my head created a cocoon of my own hot sweat in a pocket of steamy oxygen, but this was better than the alternative.

How did I get here? A few short months ago we were a normal couple, doing all the things that society said would help us live the American dream. It was safe. It was predictable. Nothing about what we were doing at this moment was remotely predictable and to anyone looking on, probably not safe either. In fact, some would say it was simply crazy.

I could feel my heartbeat pulsating, but it was due to the stifling oxygen under the blanket. This was plane travel in 1997, where Government regulations regarding smoking on international flights had not been completely abolished yet. Apparently, though we had requested the non-smoking section in the aircraft, our seats were right behind the smoking section. The thin airplane-issued blanket over my head served as my only partition between the smoke and semi-smoke-free air.

"Really? What kind of no-smoking section is this?" I gasped to my husband, Jim, between blanket folds. He squeezed my hand sympathetically.

"Maybe this is how all international flights to South America are? I have no idea. Another first to experience together."

As the small plane rocked with turbulence, my hand went to my still flat belly. The thought that I was even carrying our firstborn was a brand-new concept to me. We were the couple that was supposed to adopt. My body was not even supposed to be able to get pregnant, or at least, that's what I had been told all my life. Yet here I was, pregnant and flying over the Atlantic Ocean.

So if you had told me even three months ago that we would be on a small international plane headed into the middle of the Amazon, newly expecting our first miracle, with everything we owned in fourteen boxes in the plane's cargo hold (along with our dog and cat), I would have bet my life that you were speaking of a completely different person. Except for the plane's roller coaster turbulence, which brought me back to reality, I felt a bit like I was having an out-of-body experience.

Sometimes when you least expect it, God takes you completely out of your comfort zone, and lets you experience the impossibilities in your mind so He can grow your vision for the future that He has for you. In our case, our future was a place we only knew as a dot on our world map, Manaus, Amazonas, Brazil. We had never even heard of Manaus, but it became our new vision.

My thoughts reeled with my emotions and my body answered. Trembling with excitement, my inexperienced, adventurous twenty-four-year-old brain wouldn't even entertain the idea of fear of the unknown. There were still so many unknowns, questions we had no answers to, but ones our family and friends had voiced: "Where will you live? Will you have a car? How are you going to get around? What about health insurance? Are the doctors there equipped to handle a high-risk pregnancy? Do they even have a hospital where you are going? Maybe you should wait at least till the baby comes. Maybe this isn't the best timing right now."

We *did* have all that: a beautiful home, two cars, nice paying jobs that came with full health benefits. Those questions were not unwarranted, as within a year of being married we decided to quit our jobs, sell all our belongings, both cars, and jumped on a plane to answer a single desperate phone call for help to teach at a small school in the Amazon. Maybe we didn't have all the answers at that moment, but we knew that we had to take that step and put our faith over our fear of the unknown.

This was the biggest step of faith we had ever encountered and only after we had committed to go did we find out my latest bout of what I thought was the flu was actually pregnancy. It was a dream we had been told was impossible due to my ongoing lifetime of health issues. My doctor explained that I was extremely high risk for carrying a baby full term and there was a possibility that I could lose the baby, as they could not predict how my body would even react to a pregnancy. Now our move just brought this pregnancy to a whole other risk level.

It was only a few weeks earlier that I had broken the news to my husband that he was going to be a father. His mouth smiled, but his eyes betrayed his worry.

"Aren't you happy?" I whispered.

31

"Of course, but this changes everything!" He ran his fingers nervously through his hair. "Maybe we shouldn't go anymore. Maybe we need to cancel so we can give you the best chance possible to have this baby. I don't know if they are equipped in the Amazon to handle issues if something goes wrong."

With my hand still on my stomach, my thoughts tumbled in my head. This most certainly did change a lot of things. What were we thinking, running off to the Amazon jungle to teach kids? Leaving behind a secure structure of family, friends, doctors, and everything we had ever known? And, of course, the missionaries would have understood, as this was completely unexpected. And due to my medical history and the opinions of my doctors, it definitely would have been in my best interest to stay in the United States for this baby.

I shook my head. No, our circumstances would always change; that's life. Our lives can change day by day, hour by hour. Our response to that change is what produces steadfastness and tenacity. We could choose to operate in fear, or we could take each challenge as it came and firmly stand grounded in our faith and vision for the opportunity we knew God was giving us.

I smiled reassuringly at my husband. "They've been having babies down there for years. If they can do it, so can I. I know one thing that hasn't changed, and that's God's will. If it was His will for us to go to the Amazon yesterday, then what's changed? This baby is only an added blessing. We need to go."

Our excitement and eagerness for following our hearts and our vision overshadowed our fear of the unknown. We left behind the doubt and the many questions that crowded the good sense everyone thought we had lost in our vision for our dream life together. Was it worth it? There was only one way to find out.

The lurch of the plane as the wheels hit the tarmac broke me out of my thoughts. We had just touched down in a completely foreign land. The Portuguese welcome over the plane intercom reminded me of that fact, as did the stark realization that I had absolutely no understanding of Portuguese or any foreign language, for that matter. This was exactly why I had changed my major four times in college: to get away from having to learn a foreign language. Now I found myself in the exact opposite position of my college advisor's advice: "Never be a missionary if your brain can't handle the different languages." I smiled at the irony. I took a first deep breath of my new surroundings and thought to myself, *Let our adventure begin.*

Along with the wall of heat, 100% humidity, and the 100 degrees that was the Amazon, came hugs and warm greetings — thankfully in English — from the two American missionaries who met us. They helped us to gather our dog and cat, and our small mountain of bags and boxes, into their waiting vehicles to take us to our new accommodations within the mission compound.

A small blue concrete-block house, furnished with all the basics down to the last fork and pillowcase, became our new home. One air conditioner window unit graced the main bedroom, and it immediately became our favorite place. Our washer and dryer were on the outside of the house in

33

their own covering, as they were shared by the other teachers in the house next door. We had a home. Exploring the rest of our new residence, I walked into the shower part that made up our split bathroom and my heart stopped. A single light bulb was dangling by an exposed thin wire just above the shower stall. "Definitely not in Kansas, anymore, Toto," I mumbled as I made a mental note to be extra careful when showering.

About twenty feet from our front door was the long building that served as the school. This was convenient. There was no need for a car, as we could simply walk across the grass to our classrooms. As for leaving the compound, one of the teachers living next door invited us to join her weekly grocery trip every Thursday in her small Volkswagen bug.

Adapting to living in the Amazon came by simply jumping into the surrounding culture with an open mind. Along with the heat, several creatures welcomed us to the Amazon and initiated us into our new lifestyle. We learned very quickly to just ignore the small lizards that had already taken up residence on our walls and ceiling, as apparently they were our only bug repellent. The occasional nighttime mosquito eluded them more often than not, though, so the hanging net covering our bed was also a welcome reprieve.

Then there were the ants. These tiny little devils were everywhere, but they mostly seemed to think they owned every inch of our kitchen. Placing a glass of water on the counter to reach for ice cubes became a race, as the glass would be taken over by an almost invisible army of these itty-bitty warriors by the time we retrieved it for a sip. We learned to never put our drinks down if we wanted to finish the contents. The ants became such a nuisance to those of us living within the compound that

34

the missionaries started poisoning the ant piles around the area to try and control the issue. Unknowingly, the Brazilian nationals were collecting the ants and frying them over the fire as a delicacy for dinner each evening while attending the local Bible institute on the compound. Word spread quickly upriver that the institute had "bad ants" after a slew of stomach issues rampaged those returning to their villages.

As the Amazon introduced us to its many cultural inhabitants, my body was also painfully aware of our new environment and balked at having to adjust to the humidity, new food, and the stifling jungle heat. Taking two or three showers a day to help regulate my body temperature became my routine. The extreme humidity was a wall that kept smothering my body into breath-stealing exhaustion each day. I started losing weight at an alarming speed. Finding a good obstetrician became a priority, along with a local medical plan that could help defray the costs of my two-month-along pregnancy.

Within those first few weeks, with the missionaries' help, we were able to access Brazilian insurance despite my "pre-existing condition" (pregnancy), and unbelievably it covered my entire maternity. What a relief.

As we watched our vision become our reality, our faith increased each day as many of the answers to those questions at the beginning started to unfold before us. When we shut out the noise of those who didn't understand our decision and took that first step of faith into the unknown, we discovered that the safest place to be was right where God wanted us.

My husband, Jim, was getting ready to teach the small class of ninth and tenth graders so they wouldn't have to go up the Amazon River to a boarding school, when during his preparations we found out that one of his students was the daughter of an OBG doctor, Dr. Cibele Cabrejos. She was one of the directors of the only maternity hospital in Manaus, Brazil. I smiled to myself: *OBG doctor and hospital, two more questions answered.*

Dr. Cibele became my passport to the most personable medical hospitality I had ever experienced. Within that first month of our arrival, I had lost over twelve pounds and had become severely dehydrated. When she saw how much weight I had lost, she patted my belly assuredly, "Oh, no worry, you have parasite. It's normal," she said in her limited English.

What?! My mind automatically pictured the invading sinister parasitic worm setting up house in my belly alongside my baby. I swallowed hard. I could think of many other words to describe my situation, but *normal* was not one. She administered a deworming treatment, and I was admitted to a private room at UNIMED Maternity hospital for a weekend of rest, fluids, and nourishment. This became a routine part of my care, as I spent at least one weekend a month in the hospital for much needed nutrition to keep that parasite evicted and give my body the best chance at health throughout this high-risk pregnancy.

My classroom became my multi-cultural initiation into education; however, many times I felt more like the student than the teacher. My life was turning out completely differently than I ever imagined. Life in the

Amazon taught me strength and a resilience that I never knew I had within me.

My pregnancy was not easy, and it landed me in the hospital several more times as my body struggled to maintain a healthy weight to give birth. But seven months later, we held our miracle: a healthy, perfect, Brazilian-born daughter; and I couldn't imagine her being born anywhere else in the world.

Taking that first step is many times the hardest of all. Fear can be both a powerful motivator and a deterrent. When we allow our feelings to dictate our actions, we can mistake those emotions for a confirmation on which we base our decisions. I was so grateful we did not allow opinions or fear to guide our decision. Instead, faith is stepping out against all odds when circumstances and popular opinion seem to dictate the opposite. By getting on that plane, we had unlocked the key to an amazing path full of joy, contentment and we were experiencing our vision for the future.

I wasn't sure how big my faith was, but I did know that my dreams were still coming true. I was living an extraordinary life beyond what I could have ever imagined. Somewhere between landing in the middle of the Amazon, and holding my new daughter in my arms, I had opened my heart and embraced our future with absolute vision for what life was offering us.

About the Author

Kristina L. Foster is an American born entrepreneur, a professional graphic and interior designer, book cover designer, and has her masters in Portrait Art. She lives with her missionary husband, Jim, in Cape Town, South Africa. Her pride and joy are her two grown, beautiful miracle girls, Briana and Elise. Kristina loves to travel and has been to 48 of the 50 United States, and over 13 countries. Compelled by her own miraculous birth story, Kristina founded the first South African chapter of Now I Lay Me Down to Sleep — a non-profit organization that provides the healing gift of remembrance portraits to parents experiencing the loss of a baby.

Diagnosed with fibromyalgia, chronic fatigue and severe anemia after dealing with over 17 operations throughout her life, Kristina went on a healing journey of discovery that led her to make holistic changes in using pure essential oils to create a toxin-free lifestyle. Both a missionary and a pastor's wife, Kristina loves to share her health journey with anyone who will listen, along with coaching others on how to live a more natural lifestyle. Her love for others (and coffee) often places her in a local cafe, appearing alongside those who are searching for answers while creating long-term personal connections.

Kristina was a co-author in the international best-seller *Absolute Will,* designed the covers for *Absolute Will* and *Absolute Vision,* and is co-authoring a soon-to-be published autobiography with her father — Author, Pastor, and Historian, Dr. Ron Surels — that chronicles her life from birth to present day, detailing her quest for healing while discovering God's perfect will and testament of His saving grace over her life.

You can connect with Kristina here:

Personal Website:
KristinaSurelsFoster.com

Instagram:
https://www.instagram.com/miracle2mom/

Family Ministry website:
www.goodhopeministries.com

Email: kfphotoministries@gmail.com

CHAPTER 4

My Greatest Vision

Greta Trefalt

"I will be a ballerina," said my four-year-old self with no hesitation, no thinking — just pure heart and soul: my first love. It was a vision that chose me, and from then on it was the answer I gave whenever I was asked, "What do you want to be when you grow up?"

It didn't matter what it would take, or what I needed to sacrifice.

My neighbor took me to my first ballet class. From that day on, every Tuesday and Thursday afternoon from 4:00 p.m. to 4:45 p.m. I was in the ballet studio. I still remember the big corner building, shiny marble stairs, second floor, studio left, ballet bars, mirror, changing rooms full of excited little girls in pink leotards, smiling parents greeting each other and exchanging small talk, saying hi to my friends, and saying bye-bye to my father.

"Be good in the class," he would reply.

I would run to him after the class with wide open arms and a massive, satisfied grin at being able to find him among so many giant humans called parents. He would pick me up and give me the biggest hug in the world with lots of kisses and cuddles, as if we'd been apart for centuries, not just for one ballet class.

The best part of the experience was going to the pastry shop afterwards. I loved our weekly ritual of being together, walking through the park towards the pastry shop. I would always choose the same cake and drink. He would always get his same favorites too, and then we would take the bus home. I would name every station, all the streets we passed, and could name countries and capital cities around the world. I loved that game — it was the first indication of my deep love of traveling, even if at first traveling meant boarding an ordinary public-transport bus. I have very good orientation and can easily remember roads and shortcuts.

It was unusual in that time period to be a little girl raised by a single father. I was so often a little bit different that being different became normal for me. I was still very young when he let me go on my own to my ballet classes and these experiences made me very independent from an early age.

Ballet classes were relentless repetitions of the same movement, until our teacher was satisfied with our dancing routine. Despite dreaming of being a ballerina, I didn't even like my first ballet teacher. She was old and mean and scary. Most of the time she looked fed up and bored. The next level after recreational classes for children was preschool at the one and only vocational ballet school in Belgrade, Serbia. For a few years I endured another ballet teacher I didn't like. This one had a high-pitched tone, screaming voice, and a look that was neither friendly nor loving. She mainly focused on herself in the mirror, playing with her bangs and blowing air into her hair. While speaking to the pianist about counting the music and what speed she would like it to be, she would lose control over the students and express annoyance with the happy, chatty, and naughty children.

But even her behavior did not divert me from my dancing dream. Once I learned there was an audition for primary ballet school, I took a friend of mine by the hand and confidently walked down the road-of-no-return. In the school they checked our musicality, body condition, spine, feet, and a few other things. Though the other children were with their parents, I was with my same-age friend. I passed the audition for primary ballet school, went home and told my father I had enrolled. I had a determined vision from an early age; I cannot imagine that nowadays, but in the 1980s in Belgrade it was possible.

I was dancing my dream. I would walk on my tiptoes, skip in the street, take every second step on the stairs, and jump across puddles doing the splits in the air, thinking of ballet moves all the time. Music was constantly in my head, and I was usually humming and dancing. That was my world. Every year, half the students dropped out and only a handful stayed all the way to the final year. In my class only seven students made it to the final exam.

It was not easy going to dance classes every day after school when all my friends were going home, but I was pursuing a dream that made me happy. Every day from age seven to seventeen, I typically spent ten to twelve hours a day in sweat, bleeding feet, hurting body, joy, happiness, tears, friends, and fun on a roller coaster of feelings and emotions in relentless rehearsals. I often felt life was a perpetual rehearsal and wondered when "real life" would begin. But dancers choose a mad profession and endure the endless rehearsals because we aim to achieve the unachievable — perfection. I love performing and dancing. It is my LIFE.

I still feel sentimental and nostalgic about the good old days. At the time when I was just about to start my dancing career, in the last decade of the twentieth century, Yugoslavia, the country where I was born, changed shape and became seven countries: Slovenia, Croatia, Bosnia-Herzegovina, Montenegro, Serbia, Macedonia and Kosovo. Yugoslavia ceased to exist. This separation was a messy civil war, a lot of pain and struggle — and an experience that makes me not proud of being human.

It wasn't just the country in upheaval; *everything* changed for me at that time. The civil war had a ripple effect on everyone and everything. My family was broken and my world collapsed. The death of my beloved grandmother Hilda, who helped raise me, was one of a sequence of nightmare events in that landmark year of my life. I lost my grandmother, my country, my family house, close relatives — and the father I had known and loved from my childhood remarried. In later years he became just a faint picture of the man I had revered as my very own God Zeus, but despite the heartache, betrayal, and disappointments, I will always love him.

Being a teenager was challenging in itself, but the civil war made it more so. It was an intense period of political and economic crisis, and I felt from the core of my being that nothing in that situation was either natural or beneficial. It was not natural to experience deep hate and violence, or to live with guns, low morale, quick money, and extremes of unimaginable scale. It was not natural that in the entire grocery store the only food available was endless rows of cabbage. It was not natural going with a suitcase of money to buy a loaf of bread and, by the time you got to the shop, the money could only buy half a loaf. It was not natural that I stopped drinking milk as a child so my toddler brother could have it. At one point, the country had the highest inflation rate in world history, and it was madness. Everything was a luxury, but life had so little value. The lesson I was learning was that life had no worth, and my life was no exception.

Even when we had nothing, I still wanted to perform. I still dreamed of being a ballerina. Through dancing, I could express all my emotions — grief, love, passion, and pain — and not offend or insult anybody or anything, because dance is such a powerful yet precise language. My sorrowful heart still dripped with love whenever I danced.

I felt as though I were suffocating from the fear and desperation caused by the civil war, high inflation, extreme poverty, and trying, unsuccessfully, to adjust to the new dynamics within my family unit. Everything had changed so quickly, and it felt like my country, my family, and my life had gone from the light into the darkness. I felt like I was sinking into a black hole. The best solution I could come up with to escape my circumstances was to leave. I desperately wanted to be somewhere safe, somewhere warm by the seaside, with the sky full of stars, ready for new stars to be born.

Cyprus at that time was a rescue center for former Yugoslavs and Lebanese fleeing the dangerous civil wars in both of those countries, so I made the decision to leave my family home.

That decision came at a very high price. It was not the place for one with the artistic soul of a young ballerina. In fact, Cyprus was a desert for artists. Being underage, with no legal permission to stay, young and beautiful, with very little knowledge of English and even less of Greek, I struggled. I am absolutely sure my love for life and my eye for natural art and beauty kept me alive as my soul quietly, tenderly whispered, *I want to dance.*

I had many unfortunate experiences, about which I was silent. I don't talk about being a victim of abuse in that time and place. I was deeply depressed, didn't hold much space for the love of myself, and for many years I doubted my own experience. I have buried that experience somewhere deep, as a horrible nightmare that was not part of me but just happening through me. I had to bury it to survive.

Against all odds, I did become a ballerina. I was accepted to the Royal Academy of Dance in London, England, and supported myself due to the grace of God and the kind people who crossed my path at the time. My success seemed as unlikely as me traveling to the moon and back, but I had a dream, I had a vision, I believed it, and I achieved it. In 2002, a friend gave me a CD of Wayne Dyer, the internationally renowned "father of motivation." I was determined to learn English as fluently as my mother tongue, so I could understand and follow in-depth seminars and be able to express myself in another language. I had tears in my eyes as I graduated from the Royal Academy of Dance in London as a qualified dance teacher, and later that year met Wayne Dyer himself in person.

My passion for travel and my profession as a dancer and teacher gave me the chance to travel and teach around the world, to experience the Anglo-

Saxon and Celtic cultures of Great Britain; West, East and Central Europe; India, Pakistan, and Arabia; the East Asian cultures of Singapore, China, Malaysia, Macao, Vietnam, Cambodia, and Bali; the Aboriginal culture in Australia; and the culture of indigenous native Americans of North America. I have fulfilled my vision of dancing, teaching, and traveling. I am privileged to have seen the world not as a tourist but as a citizen of the world, with purpose and mission. I know my soul has been touched so many times by kindness and love, and I hope I have touched the souls of many in return.

The last wish of my dying grandmother Hilda had been for me to plant two cypress trees on her grave. For nearly thirty-three years after her passing, I couldn't do it. I wanted to but because I loved her so much, and because of how chaotic my life was during the time when she passed, I was reluctant to accept the painful reality of her death. In 2021, I tried but failed to follow through on planting those trees, but this year while on errands in Belgrade with my father and brother (a rare event), I decided I should go to a garden center.

At that very moment, a man appeared on the street carrying two cypress trees. I ran after him, asked him where I could buy such trees, and rather than telling me where to get them, he gave them to me.

It became clear I needed to follow through this time on my grandmother's last wish. Now that I had the trees, I was decisive, determined, prepared, and ready to honor that. With my father and brother witnessing this magical synchronicity of events and the perfect alignment of support from above, it was a magical moment of unity. We planted the cypress trees in September 2022.

The appearance of the cypress trees for my grandmother was a reminder of the immense power of the universe to achieve our heartfelt desires. When I was finally ready, in my heart, the universe presented me with the trees I needed. Despite the turmoil, chaos, danger, loss, and disappointment I experienced in my life, I have chosen to be a visionary, not a victim. The power is in having one great vision after another until the greatest one arrives. My latest greatest vision is to manifest such abundance as to make a significant difference to the world around me. I see myself happily and harmoniously giving and receiving with every cell of my body, every day becoming the best version of myself, and showing others how to become the best versions of themselves.

We are indefinite, radiant light. Our hearts contain the seeds of love and joy, and by some miracle we are together in space and time on this single planet in a vast universe. I am here to manifest and share the experience of abundant joy and vision. That is my greatest vision. What is yours?

About the Author

"Born in the world, not of this world."

Greta Trefalt was born in Belgrade, Yugoslavia, and traveled with her grandparents around Europe as a child. She settled in Belgrade again while she learned ballet, lived in Cyprus due to the civil war in her homeland, and then moved to London for her higher education.

After dancing professionally, Greta was accepted to the Royal Academy of Dance in London, where she obtained her Professional Teaching Dancing Diploma. She has worked internationally in London, Singapore, and China as a teacher of ballet and yoga, and was artistic director for an international dance school in China. Her work centers around teaching, coaching, mentoring, lecturing — anything she can do to help people get to the next level of success, in every aspect of life. She is an expert in health and fitness with a holistic approach to healing. She conducts classes in yoga, meditation, massage and aromatherapy.

Greta enjoys traveling and immersing herself in world cultures, connecting with people professionally, personally, and on a soul level. She is happiest while conducting her "soul business" through retreats around the world, sharing her knowledge, skills, experience, enthusiasm, and insights. Her dearest family consists of her many close friends around the world.

She has worked as a volunteer in Kosovo, Pakistan and Sri Lanka after natural disasters, has conducted classes for an orphanage, and has helped with fundraising for Kampala, Uganda.

Greta can be reached here:

Website:
https://gretatrefalt.com/

Email: gretatrefalt@yahoo.com

CHAPTER 5

Outside Looking In

Jennifer D. Scharf

A s I got ready for work that first day, I was filled with excitement. My vision to make a difference for at-risk students in the local school district was strong. I became a certified educator in special education to support diverse learners as I, too, was neurodivergent. So I felt prepared and ready for the challenges that lay ahead on that first day.

Opening those school doors, however, I was hit with a long-forgotten smell that instantly made my stomach rise into my throat. Sweaty kids, cleaning solution, chalk, paper, pencils, glue... the typical school odors had me fighting to keep down the contents of that morning's breakfast. Until that very moment, I hadn't even realized schools have a particular smell, but they do.

As I was standing there frozen, shaking, and sweating profusely, I realized I was having a full-on anxiety attack. *Why was I standing in the doorway like a deer in the headlights? How could this be happening?* I had no idea my own negative experiences in school were so traumatizing until I was hit with PTSD.

I had somehow blocked out and forgotten my past school trauma, my inadequacies, and all the failures I had in school. But now on my first day of work, flashing before my eyes, I could see every corner I'd ever stood in, and I could hear old Mrs. Clark's voice screeching, "What's wrong with you?" as she shook me with her iron grip until I had left a puddle on the floor. My inability to concentrate in class, follow direction, and learn like my peers often had me in her "bad books."

Following these destructive incidents in grade two were many challenging years that left me feeling inadequate and wondering why I couldn't be like everyone else in my class. I didn't understand why I struggled, and I, too, often questioned what *was* wrong with me?

As I stood there in the doorway reliving my past trauma, my vision to advocate for diverse learners became stronger and clearer than ever. No child should experience what I had gone through because of their different learning style, and I was determined to make a difference. I pulled myself together and stepped into the school. Right then and there, I knew working for the school district was going to be a wild ride, so I held on tight and trusted that I knew what I was doing. I knew I had what it took, because through my own adversity as a unique learner, I developed the mindset to never give in and never give up. With absolute determination and a clear vision driving me forward, I was going to be successful. I was right where I was meant to be, challenging my trauma, facing my fears, and fighting for equitable education for students who were *different* just like me.

Looking back on this now, it's nothing short of a miracle that I made it through that first day of work and that I continued working in the British Columbia public education system for the following twenty years. Those years were significant, as they were filled with many student successes, but they were also challenging because I supported an atypical group of students who often struggled to fit in mainstream education. As a divergent learner, I whole-heartedly related to the experiences of my students struggling to fit in a system that was designed for the neurotypical. Most of my younger years in education were spent failing in an environment that wasn't designed to support my unique learning needs. And not fitting into one's environment, or feeling like your environment doesn't support you, can have disastrous effects on a person's psyche.

Realizing I was different and that I didn't fit into my school environment was a shock. I didn't even know I was neurodivergent because my family supported my high-spiritedness and unusual passions, from creature hunting to playing in the mud and exploring the world as if I were a wood nymph. I felt included by my parents and siblings as they always seemed interested in my latest adventures. And they were especially curious about what critters I would bring home. From snakes to fawns, I always had some new creature with me to share with the family. This different way to connect with my environment didn't seem unusual to them or to me at the time. In fact, I needed this tactile way of connecting with my environment to understand how to engage with it. My family seemed to understand this, as they nurtured my unique nature, so I had never questioned my atypical ways.

As I grew older, my differences became more apparent. Both my brother and sister were above average in school, very social, had large friend groups, and had several common interests with each other. Their favorite late-night talk shows, Archie comics, and MAD magazines — the ones filled with parodies and laden with satire — went completely over my head. Their way to interact with our environment was possibly the first sign I was different. But in my family I was supported, valued, and loved for who I was.

It wasn't until I went to school that I realized just how my diversity would impact my development. Because my brain sees and experiences the world differently than my peers, I didn't adjust well to the classroom routine. I struggled to sit still, I couldn't concentrate, and following directions was a major challenge. I always felt like my senses were on hyperdrive; a foot tapping, the squeak of a chair, or even a cough or sniffle would have me turned around in my seat searching for the disrupter. At one point I believed that I had some sort of bionic hearing ability, as I could clearly hear the whispers in the back of the class. Unfortunately, because I spent more time listening to the secret whispers of my classmates, recalling and reciting the teacher's lessons were often impossible for me.

My success in the education system was determined by my ability to sit still, listen to the lessons, and then recall the learning. This did not suit my learning needs; without a tactile learning environment where I could physically move, touch, and engage, years of opportunity for my foundational learning were lost. My grades suffered, my self-esteem declined, and for many years I was an underachiever. I didn't reach my learning capacity because my educational environment excluded me.

The education system often keeps us neurodivergent learners locked out from accessing our learning in many ways. Essentially, the system is designed with gatekeepers upholding the structure, and without the right key — or learning style — we are statistically less likely to get through.

Many of us don't graduate and even fewer of us attend post-secondary education. It's not that we aren't as intelligent; we just access our brains differently and often need learning embedded in concrete examples with opportunities to engage with the material in multiple ways. Sadly, the neurotypical system left me feeling defeated, as I could not engage with my environment in the way that I knew how, and therefore was often left standing on the outside of my academic setting looking in.

Against the odds, I managed to graduate from high school, and I went on to university. My vision to be on the inside of the academic world, and my mindset to never give in and never give up, drove my success. Fighting through this system, though, wasn't without its setbacks and challenges. So many times through my first few years of university I felt queasy and on the verge of either passing out or throwing up, usually right before I had an assignment handed back. My heart would race, my palms would start to sweat, and I could feel the skin prickle on the back of my neck as I turned over my paper to peer at my mark. It felt like I was entering a dark alley, waiting for some sort of impending doom. This was multi-layered fear; fear that I would fail the assignment and fear that I wasn't cut out to be a university student. Waiting for that "F," which was in fact an exit ticket and the loss of one's seat in a university class, was my impending doom. As time went on, though, my marks improved, but even to this day, whenever I flip over an assignment I still experience a spike in adrenaline that sends a shiver up my spine and my heart racing.

Although my first few years in university weren't overly successful, I discovered I excelled in areas I connected with. I entered a program that certified students to support those with diverse abilities and realized I was in my element. Because of my own struggles, I connected with the content and understood the significance of supporting others who experience challenges.

However, being on the Dean's List, a top achiever in my program, prompted me to question the reality of my own learning "inability." My poor grades and learning challenges as a child made me believe there was something wrong with me: a disability or deficit that prevented me from thriving in an academic environment. But now my high achievement in this program had me questioning my experiences and the entire structure of the education system.

Atypical learners have grown so accustomed to being *the problem* or source of the pathology that we often don't even question the system that oppresses us. And being told to access disability services because of our unique learning needs perpetuates a system that blames the learner for being different. Years of education and experience in working with divergent learners have helped me to understand that it's not the individual with the diverse ability who needs to change; it's the system which is the source of our oppression. This backwards, blame-the-learner perspective was the catalyst that drove me to challenge this ideology, instilling a vision in me to advocate for myself and to push for change. This mindset led to my success in education and was the key to get past the gatekeepers.

After graduating from post-secondary studies, my life during the years with the school district were fulfilling and meaningful. In fact, life was quite blissful for many years. I met and married my best friend. And when our two girls came along, we moved to the country to raise them. After a long hiatus from academic learning, I returned to university and took night classes to upgrade my education in the social service field, as I continued to be drawn to understanding better ways of how to support atypical and at-risk individuals.

Although I was skilled to overcome adversity in many ways, I wasn't prepared for the loss of my husband in 2014. My mental and physical health were significantly impacted, and my children's needs were all I could manage. My vision to empower and advocate for change for the neurodiverse ceased as my family's life changed forever and my world imploded. I retired from the school district and drew inward to find the strength to move forward and heal.

At forty, I became a widow and a solo parent. I didn't feel old enough to have my happily-ever-after ripped away from me, and helplessly watching him fade from our lives almost killed me. By age forty-five, I weighed under one hundred pounds as I developed an autoimmune disorder from the trauma. And unfortunately, the treatments prescribed by multiple specialists failed to improve my condition. Living in pain for over five years made me want to give up, but my family needed me. I had raised two incredibly strong, independent daughters, and they still needed me to show them how to survive through tragedy.

Although I continued to face many health challenges, I returned fulltime to university as a way to survive. I used it as my treatment since it helped me move forward. It was my atypical personality, however, that pushed me to continue to fulfill my many ambitions: I completed my degree, obtained a teaching certificate, and shortly thereafter my daughters and I developed a teaching company to support at-risk students during the pandemic. In many ways the world was shutting down around us, but we knew how to survive through adversity, and we knew how to fulfill a need and make a difference.

In 2020, I was on a new therapy and my body finally began to heal. Years of researching and advocating for my health finally paid off as I never gave in nor gave up. This renewed health prompted me to again return to university; this time, to complete a Master of Education degree. In my teaching practice I continue to support at-risk students falling through the cracks — thus, the drive to support diverse learners persists. Knowing the challenges these students face, I know I need to do more to make a difference. Therefore, my journey to be their advocate must continue.

Having the absolute vision to challenge defeat while facing multiple adversities has been a prolific force in my life. My determination to never give in and never give up has been the key to my many successes. More importantly, continuing with my own education has helped guide me through the darkest days as it reignited my drive and realigned my vision for supporting atypical learners.

My journey is far from over, however, as even now, I'm still faced with multiple barriers navigating through the neurotypical world of academia. Thus, my work in understanding how to be a driver of change often feels like it's just begun. My fight to support equitable education for diverse learners will continue because all learners deserve to stand on the inside of the academic world instead of on the outside looking in.

About the Author

Jennifer D. Scharf is a teacher and an academic writing tutor for diverse learners in both grade school and upper-level university. She currently lives in Kelowna, British Columbia, Canada, with her youngest daughter Taylor while commuting to Kamloops for work and to upgrade her education. She has a Human Service Work Certificate, a degree in Social Work, an English Language Teaching Certificate and as of early 2023 is currently entering her last semester of her Master of Education degree.

Her love of culture and travel often has her abroad searching for new adventures and meaningful ways to connect with the world. She is a sculptor and pottery teacher in her spare time and her tactile interest in her environment still has her playing in the mud, as she is often digging in clay beds across the globe.

Both Jenn's adult daughters are driven by their own pursuits in equitable education, as they are strongly influenced by their mother's passion in this field. Her eldest daughter Sidney, who lives in Burnaby, British Columbia, has her degree with a major in Asian studies, a minor in education and is currently a teacher working with English language learners. Taylor also has a strong interest in culture and is pursuing a career in education through the University of British Columbia-Okanagan.

Jenn has spent the majority of her career advocating and fighting for equitable education for the divergent learner. Her current research on exploring the post high-school barriers for neurodivergent learners gives voice to the experiences of other atypical learners and provides evidence-based rationale for systemic change.

Through research and her future publications, it is her hope that expanding public awareness will narrow the gap in equitable access to post high-school success and reduce socioeconomic and health disparities for divergent learners. She continues to pursue a career in equitable education at the post-secondary level and plans to enter a Special Education doctoral program once her master's degree is complete.

Jenn is grateful to all who have contributed to her journey on becoming an educator, and now a published author. In addition to the love and support received by her daughters, both of her parents, Herb and Cheryl, and her siblings, Tracy and Randy, have contributed in many ways to Jenn's success in education over the years and continue to support her career in advocating for at-risk students. She is thankful for Cory and Melanie, who have opened their home and hearts to her while she completes her master's degree, and she is indebted to Dr. Karen Densky, who planted the seed, believed in her and supported her while she grew.

You can connect with Jenn here:

Website:
https://thelanguageeducators.com/

Instagram:
https://www.instagram.com/jennscharf/

CHAPTER 6

Navigating My New Normal

Christina Carlos

Have you ever wondered if someone, or something, is trying to tell you something? Or if things happen for a reason? This thought has plagued me ever since I explained to a spiritual acupuncturist that I have been in four car accidents. It is not very often you meet or hear of someone who has been hit so many times. He said the universe had been trying to get my attention, and unfortunately, I had not been listening.

Accident number three happened more than five years ago, yet I still feel the shock and fear as if it were yesterday. I had just gotten married the week prior, on New Year's Eve, and my husband and I were getting ready to leave for our honeymoon. My teenage daughter and I had decided to go for a drive and spend a bit of time together before my trip away. It was a cold January day, with the odd snowflake falling from the sky, and as she turned the car onto the highway, she started to slow down for a red light up ahead. I will never forget the look on her face as she realized the car was going to hit us from the side. I can still hear her screaming, I can still see the cement highway barrier coming towards us, I can remember the volunteer firefighter helping us get out of the car, I can remember trying to calm my daughter down, letting her know we were okay.

But actually, I wasn't okay. Within hours of the accident my body started to ache, and bruises started to show up. Those were just the injuries you could see. Call it intuition or a gut feeling, but I knew something was physically wrong with me after this accident, and that I might not fully recover from it. Getting up the next morning to catch our flight was difficult and I could not even lift my five-pound carry-on bag. It certainly wasn't the romantic getaway my new husband and I had been looking forward to. I spent our two-week honeymoon heavily dosed on anti-inflammatory medication and pain relievers, while doing as little as possible.

I have congenital spondylolisthesis in my lower back, specifically in the L5/S1 area. Many people may have this condition and not even realize it, as it may not cause any pain or discomfort at all. I had never let it slow me down. I was a very independent person who lived to be outdoors, and it was something I looked forward to almost daily. Running was a huge part of my life for many years, and I would often run at least four or five times per week. Being outside and active was my vice, the one thing I needed to do to help alleviate my stress levels and to feel free. I would feel at peace during and after a run, and it gave me a sense of accomplishment. Being a mother (and a single mom for many years) meant my family often came first, but when I went for a run it was my time, something just for me.

Only two years earlier, my second accident, a rear-ender, had made me hang up my running shoes, although I was able to remain active in other aspects. I could still get my feeling of peace and freedom from hiking, kayaking, and going for long walks. Just after that second accident, I had gone to see a physiatrist to determine if the spondylolisthesis had worsened and, if so, what I could do to help it. He had warned me then to avoid any further car accidents if possible, so he was a bit shocked to see me only two years later, having just been in accident number three.

I haven't had an easy life, yet I have always tried to look at what was good, to remain as positive as possible, and admittedly I've always been the worst at asking others for any help. Asking for help would mean I wasn't capable of doing things myself, and I have always been the textbook definition of independent. That third accident changed everything, and I knew soon after it happened that I would need to make some major adjustments in my life. I needed to start thinking about myself.

So I spent my time around the pool in Mexico completing a business plan and deciding on a business name for my own company. When we returned to Canada, I began implementing my plan: registering my business name and setting the parameters in place for when I could no longer work full time. That time came much sooner than I had anticipated. Unfortunately, I had deteriorated rapidly.

Prior to the major accident, I worked full time at an accounting office as a bookkeeper, and within days of returning home I had to take another week off to try to recover. I was not able to sit at my desk for very long due to the immense pain in my lower back, hips and down my legs, and I had started to notice it was getting harder for me to walk for very long at a time. The pain did not abate enough for me to return to work, which forced me to leave my full-time job — my reliable income source — by the end of February 2017.

It was a very scary time. Within that year, I went from being an independent, active woman, excited about a new marriage and the new life we were building, to not being able to walk more than one block because of severe pain. My spondylolisthesis had slipped forward and the sciatic nerves serving both my legs were being crushed.

Thirteen months after my third accident, I underwent a six-hour spinal fusion surgery to stabilize the area and take the pressure off the nerves. My previous life of going for a long run, enjoying views from an amazing hike, and not having to rely on anyone was gone.

I was in constant pain, and yet I tried my best to hide it from the people around me, including my family. I know I did not do a very good job at that, though, despite trying to keep a smile on my face every day. The hardest thing for me to accept was no longer being a strong, independent woman who could do things on her own.

I realized I had two choices: 1. I could dwell on my injuries, the emotional trauma from the car accidents and dive into a deep depression, or 2. I could figure out a way to navigate my new normal and accept the physical rehabilitation I needed and will continue to need in the years ahead. Did I want to dwell on all the negatives in my life? Not one bit. My fierce competitiveness from all the years of being an athlete reared its head and I wouldn't allow myself to admit defeat. I was not going to let these moments, these unwanted injuries, these car accidents, determine my life. But I also had to eat some humble pie and come to terms with the fact that I was going to have to start asking for help.

Talking about my feelings and how these car accidents have affected me is very difficult. I am not one to be negative or admit when something is wrong. I also tend to avoid admitting I am in pain. My fear is if I allow any space for negative thoughts or spend any time thinking about how much pain I'm really in or what could have been a tragic outcome, I will end up in a dark place from which I won't come back. My focus has always been that I'm grateful to be alive, and grateful my daughter is alive.

But I now must learn to live with intense pain, anger, and other feelings I've never had before, and it is scary. I have troubling anxieties from the third accident, but other emotions are even harder to deal with: guilt because I allowed my daughter to drive that day and she could have been seriously hurt, and grief for the loss of the activities I can no longer do and had long taken for granted. I have had to grieve losing my independence.

To be honest, many days I wanted to give up, cry on the couch and play the "why me" card. Doctors recommended I shouldn't work for at least a year after surgery and informed me I will most likely always have nerve pain. But I could not afford a year with no income. Our blended family included four children at home, so going down to just my husband's income would have made things extremely tight. I had to figure out how to set up my new business in such a way as to find the perfect work-life-rehab balance, to allow my body to heal and still earn an income. I needed flexibility in my day-to-day life, so when I had my not-so-good days (which were many), I could take the time I needed to let my body heal.

Luckily for me, I already had many years of experience helping other business owners, and I knew where to find the tools I needed to guide me in the right direction. I had an idea of what this new business was going to look like, and the steps I needed to take. The first step was to develop a rough outline of a business plan to figure out my goals, and then make good decisions to reach those goals.

Starting a new business is much like planning to drive somewhere. You need to know your destination (the vision for your business) and then determine the best route to take (your monthly or yearly goals). Without a plan and a map, you will likely get lost along the way.

For the first few years, I worked on my own, hired a few great subcontractors to help me from time to time, and my clients understood I could not be at my desk full time. In my free time, I took many courses and webinars, adding to my skills and knowledge to help me become a better business owner and bookkeeper for my clients. This knowledge gave me the additional tools I needed to build a solid foundation for my business, but I was still struggling with my limitations and with reaching the goals I had set for myself.

It was difficult to stay motivated every day when I had so many personal setbacks, including a fourth car accident only a few months after my back surgery. I was in pain most of the time and my business plan was starting to gather dust in the corner, but I couldn't give up. I knew I needed to be patient and stick to my plan, but I also knew I needed to brush it off, review it, and make some adjustments.

I had to find the balance between trying to work on client files and not overdoing it to the point of no return regarding my pain tolerance. Chronic pain takes a toll on your nervous system and can make you feel exhausted. It's been a challenge to manage at times. There were many, many frustrations I had to overcome and many times I had wanted to give up. But I kept going. I'm not sure where this strength comes from; maybe it's my stubbornness, or maybe I just don't want to fail. Thankfully, I had the support I needed in my home life to help me keep going, but I needed that support in my business as well.

One of the best decisions I made was to bring on a likeminded partner who had the same dreams as I did about where we could take this business. We had a friendship spanning almost thirty years, knew each other very well and had the same ideologies: we wanted to build a busy, successful business without sacrificing everything else; we wanted to offer the best client work possible yet not be tied to our desks. This balance would allow us to keep enjoying our lives, our hobbies and our families as much as possible, and give me time off for therapy appointments and recovery while still maintaining a full client list that would generate a steady income to support us and our company.

We rebranded and morphed my rough business plan into a much better five-year model with clear, tangible steps for us to take in the right direction. We have since implemented checklists and put processes and systems in place to ensure we stick to our goals and are properly set up for future growth.

Our partnership allowed me to work around my injuries and today the business is thriving. We have expanded and hired employees, booked more clients, and the business is quickly growing each month. I work with some amazing people, and we have a vision to become one of the largest virtual bookkeeping firms in British Columbia, Canada. I still have days when I need to take a break and rest my body, but I enjoy the work I do and the people I work with, both inside and outside our organization. It brings me joy to see other business owners reach their goals and become successful, and I am hoping we can impart our ever-expanding knowledge and skills to help other business owners achieve the work-life balance we have found to be so valuable to us.

I have tried my best to accept the injuries I sustained, but not dwell on them. I will never be able to lace up a pair of running shoes again or know what it is like to not be in pain. I still must endure physiotherapy and other treatments on a weekly basis and keep up my daily physical rehabilitation exercises, and yes, I still need to ask for help. But I have come to accept new things in my world, and I try to keep smiling most days.

I have spent quite a bit a time deciphering the spiritual acupuncturist's comments and I have come to realize sometimes we need to take a breath and stop for a minute. It is easy to get caught up in our daily "hustle and bustle" and forget what is most important in life. Sometimes it takes a major life change to give us vision and clarity.

There is something to it when people say you can either make lemonade with the lemons you have been given, or you can dwell on how sour they are. I chose to take a life-changing negative situation and make something positive out of it. Would I have started my own business if I had not been injured so seriously? Probably at some point, but certainly not when I did. I needed that push, and my injuries gave me the incentive to create something that worked for me. I knew what I wanted, and no roadblocks were going to get in my way. Creating my own business meant I was finally able to do something for myself again.

About the Author

Christina Carlos, B.A., CPB, received her Bachelor of Arts in Leisure Service Administration from the University of Victoria, in British Columbia, Canada and then proceeded to work in many different areas including recreational facilities, extended care homes and youth programs for the first part of her career. These opportunities allowed her to enjoy such things as rock-climbing, white-water rafting, kayaking, and team-building activities including high- and low-ropes courses.

After staying at home to raise her two daughters, Christina then changed her focus to helping small business owners with their bookkeeping and administration, finally pursuing bookkeeping full-time in 2014. This still allowed her to connect with people and hear the stories of how they started their own business. She is a QuickBooks ProAdvisor, advanced certified in QuickBooks Online and QuickBooks Desktop, is a Certified Professional Bookkeeper and active member of CPB Canada and is a certified tax preparer. With over fifteen years' experience in this field, her main focus is to help incorporations and small businesses achieve their business goals and be successful in their own right.

These days, when she is not in her office, Christina loves to be outdoors, either camping, going for a walk on the local trails, on the lake in the family boat, or tending to her vegetable garden. She also loves to travel, will not say no to a glass of red wine, and loves to spend time in her kitchen trying out a new recipe or dish. She also loves to spend as much time as possible with her family and friends.

You can connect with Christina here:

Website:
https://www.karvesolutions.ca/

Phone: (250) 709-4188 ext. 1

LinkedIn:
https://www.linkedin.com/in/christina-carlos-cpb-0b0314159/

Email: christina@karvesolutions.ca

CHAPTER 7

Supernatural

Nathan Pendleton

When someone asks me what I do for a living, my face lights up and my heart smiles. People love to know what on earth makes a successful charter-fishing captain give up his lifelong dream and move to Nicaragua, the land of lakes and volcanoes, the second poorest country in the western hemisphere, a country riddled with a tumultuous past, where nearly 70% of the population lives on two dollars a day or less. I mean, who gives up their boyhood dream and moves to a country most are trying desperately to escape from?

I was raised in a large family of nine and my life has been anything but normal. Starting in kindergarten, my siblings and I all attended Christian school fulltime, and we went to church every single time the doors were open. Sunday morning, Sunday night, Wednesday night, vacation Bible school, revival meetings — our lives revolved around the church. It's ironic to have circled back to what I'm doing now, because between then and now I was always the black sheep, the "one that got off the path," as my mom would say.

My teenage years were rough. I didn't just accept what I was being taught by the church and school. I could see the hypocrisy, and it made my skin crawl. The beginning of my sophomore year was the breaking point, though. I was tired of being told, "Because I said so," and, "Because the bible says to respect your elders," and "You don't have the right to ask questions." I had trouble conforming, was quickly labeled the bad guy and kicked out of the private high school I had been attending for breaking their code of conduct on multiple occasions. This may seem trivial, but it's devastating when it's everything you have ever known. My lifelong friends were no longer allowed to talk to me.

This only compounded the existing problems between my father and me. Don't get me wrong, I loved him deeply. He loved my mom better than I have seen any other man love his wife. But when you "spank" me with a piece of wood 150 times and call it love, something is terribly wrong. When I can't sit on the toilet, sit in a chair, or lie down on my back for several days after, well, that's just abuse.

After graduating from the local public high school, I left for the United States Army at the ripe old age of seventeen and was in boot camp when I turned eighteen. I served as a combat medic in the 2nd Battalion, 505th Parachute Infantry Regiment, 82nd Airborne Division based in Fort Bragg, North Carolina, until receiving a medical discharge in 2004. From there I moved to Jacksonville, Florida, and began working at Baptist hospital as an anesthesia technician. I also enrolled at the University of North Florida and graduated in 2008 with a Bachelor of Business Administration degree, right as the economy crashed. I had envisioned becoming a medical-device salesman and making the big bucks but, unfortunately, I was competing with others that had ten-plus years of sales experience with giants like Johnson & Johnson. So, three years after graduating, I accepted an opportunity to work for a distributor as an independent contractor.

I never drank much or did drugs in high school, but during my time in the military I began to drink heavily and regularly. I mean, how can you not when you are living in the barracks with five hundred of your brothers in arms? It's what you do. But that carried over once I was discharged, and by then I was using alcohol, marijuana, and other drugs to deal with PTSD; deal with disappointed family and friends; deal with broken relationships, including a divorce; deal with stress; and just deal with life itself.

We all know how brutal life can be. It didn't help that I did not surround myself with positive influences. I hung out at bars and ran from my problems. I didn't set out to become an addict, but I thought I was okay because I was high functioning. I had a job, a house, a boat, a dog, friends, and money to spend. The problem was that I could only deal with so much and after my divorce, losing my medical-device sales job, and then my dad passing away after I hadn't spoken to him for months, I broke. I began to use cocaine daily, along with alcohol, marijuana, LSD, mushrooms, molly, and ecstasy.

I didn't care anymore. I needed to block the pain and heartache.

It was during this time I decided to chase a lifelong dream of becoming a charter-fishing captain. I mean, what else did I have to lose at this point? I loved fishing, boats, the ocean, and had made several friends in the industry while living in Jacksonville Beach, Florida. So I went to sea school, got my captain's license, and began to work on a charter in St. Augustine, FL.

I loved the way being a boat captain made me feel. I felt like I had finally found my place in this world and could be who I wanted. But I was also still struggling with drugs. I was in fact the black sheep, the person that everyone expected me to be. A disappointment. It was "my lot in life." It was only a matter of time before I would mess it up, and I did just that.

I got arrested and charged with felony DUI (driving under the influence) and criminal mischief for dune-buggy jumping with my truck over piles of mulch on someone's private property. Too many drinks and too much cocaine will make a man do some stupid things, and I had put my captain's license, career, and freedom at risk.

It wasn't waking up in jail that shook me. It wasn't facing two felonies. It wasn't the divorce or the loss of my dad, or even a combination of all these things. It wasn't what you would guess.

One evening while lying in bed, I felt more alone and broken than ever. I always wanted to do what was right, but it seemed I never could. I didn't know where to turn for help. I didn't know what I was doing. I was lost and falling fast. At that moment I remembered my mom saying to me, "Nathan, I don't know what to say or do to help you. Someday you will need this. I don't know when, but I hope when you do you will remember this: trust in the Lord with all your heart, and do not lean on your own understanding. In all your ways acknowledge him, and he will make your paths straight." I knew these verses verbatim. I had memorized them, knew all the catechisms, stories, people, and places of the Bible. I grew up with it. It was just head knowledge, though, and not in my heart, which was exactly what I told God that very night when I made the commitment that if he was listening, if he would fix my life, I would do whatever he wanted me to do. What followed was the single most important moment in my life.

Instantly it felt as though a supernatural presence entered my room and rested on me. I could not lift my head, arms, or legs. It was heavy, almost crushing, but in a good way. I began to cry. Not like a man, but like a baby. Ugly cry. Like, really ugly. I had snot coming from my nose and I began sweating profusely from every pore in my body. I began to have visions of my childhood, teenage years, military years, and my twenties. I began to mumble over and over "forgive me, Father." I could see my dad beating me, the fights and arguments, the disappointment, the hurt everyone had endured because of me. It was almost unbearable as I cried and cried and cried while begging forgiveness from everyone. I was undone, overwhelmed, and broken beyond measure.

I awoke the next afternoon, sixteen hours later, soaking wet with sweat. To be honest, I didn't know what had happened. I thought to myself, *Wow, that was strange. I really need to quit doing so many drugs.* Even my roommate, Matt, said he had heard me crying the night before and had peered into my room. He, too, thought maybe I had just done some bad LSD.

But something in me had shifted. Something was different. I didn't notice right away, but over the next few weeks the addictions that had bound me so tight were falling away one by one. I lost interest in going to bars, chasing women, alcohol, and drugs. Instead of masking my pain through them, I would feel their emptiness.

I felt ... free.

Strangely enough, though, God had already been present. My roommate's boss, Billy, owned a landscaping company and Matt worked for him. Billy had invited me to church and, to not be rude, I had said yes and had gone with him a few times. I would drink, sniff cocaine, and smoke weed all day, every day, but on Thursdays I would come home, shower, smoke a bunch of weed and then go to church with Billy and Matt. I needed to smoke weed to feel comfortable with being in church again, even though this experience was different: the people there loved me as a person. No one told me not to come anymore until I quit using drugs. Billy had come from a similar background of drugs and alcohol but had found freedom after he had a radical encounter as well. He could see my struggles and could relate. I knew church people could probably smell marijuana on me, but they accepted me regardless.

The good part of this story is just beginning, though. Matt had also been driving the night we got arrested and charged with DUIs and Matt's job was driving one of Billy's trucks. Needless to say, Billy was upset with both of us, and I felt bad Matt could no longer drive. Fortunately, I was able to still drive under a restricted license, as this was my first offense. Because it was my off-season from fishing and I needed extra money to deal with my pending DUI charges, I had told Billy I would drive the truck so Matt could continue working and Billy wouldn't lose business. Little did I know this decision to help Billy would change my life forever.

My clarity didn't just start with my "come to Jesus" moment in my bedroom. It has become clear to me now God had already at work long before my encounter with his Holy Spirit. I felt closely guided from that point forward in dealing with everything from my DUI to working for Billy. I worked for him for the next few months, and in the process became free from all my addictions. I stayed faithful to the deal I made with God that if he fixed my life, I would do whatever he wanted me to do, and it has proved over and over to be the best deal I have ever made.

Billy and his wife were adopting two kids from Nicaragua, and the requirements included going there and fostering the kids for four to six months. Billy needed someone to run his landscaping business while he was gone. My initial reaction when he asked me was NOOOOOO! Landscaping in Florida during summer is one of the hottest jobs in the world. I fought the idea for weeks, but one Saturday Billy called me to help him finish a landscaping cleanup job.

As we were loading palm branches into a trailer to take to the dump, I came to the realization that God had been fixing my life. Considering all the ways in which my life was getting better, I could not deny it. So, I told Billy I felt like I was being led to run his business and that I would do just that. There we were, two grown men crying and hugging it out on the sidewalk. I can only imagine what people in the neighborhood thought at the sight of us.

This commitment would bring about the new life that was in store for me. During the adoption process, Billy took me on two trips to Nicaragua where things came into focus clearly and personally. As we stood in the middle of an orphanage, God told me I was "home." I thought God had lost his mind. On the second trip, Billy and I went to a little town in northern Nicaragua called Jinotega to visit a different orphanage and ministry, and I had clear visions of helping this ministry long-term. I knew it was what I needed to be doing.

After finishing my year-and-a-half work commitment to Billy, I went to Nicaragua as a volunteer for six months, to help kids living in a trash dump. It became powerfully clear to me that I was being guided, and this was my mission. One afternoon, the Holy Spirit came to me and said something that finally gave me vision for the life He wanted to give me: "Nathan, I want you to come here and help poor people." I always have the same reaction to these encounters: ugly crying.

It was simple and straight to the point, and by now it had become easier to obey. I went back to the United States with no clue how to do what I knew I needed to be doing. Through a series of events allowing the pieces to fall into place, I met a lawyer who decided to start a not-for-profit organization for me free of charge. In February 2016, just two months after leaving Nicaragua, I founded Deeply Rooted Grounds, with the sole purpose of "helping the poor." In April of that year, I moved to Nicaragua with a backpack and two duffel bags, and my mom was our organization's only financial donor.

During my previous trips to Nicaragua, I had met a beautiful young woman and we had fallen in love. Shortly after my arrival, we were married, and in the slum where she grew up we began to feed three kids a day: offering them rice, beans, and a tortilla. Three turned into seven, seven into eighteen, and eighteen turned into three hundred and fifty in what is now called The Dream Center, which also offers after-school education, medical checkups, dental checkups, a pregnant mothers club, and so much more. We also run a network of programs across the northern region of Nicaragua, feeding thousands of kids. And this is just a glimpse of my vision.

Since turning my life around, my absolute vision has always been fixed upon what I feel I've been called to do, and what God is doing in me, through me, and around me. My wife and I now have two boys of our own, and my life gets more amazing and more unbelievable every single day. I could have never imagined the life I live today, the beautiful family I get to love, and the joy of partnering with sponsors and donors from around the world to help the poorest of the poor leave poverty behind.

About the Author

Nathan Pendleton is a Colorado, United States native and the founder of Deeply Rooted Grounds, a *for-impact* organization in Central America, specifically home-based in Jinotega, Nicaragua. Nathan is the Executive Director for operations in Central America and most importantly, leads by serving the poor and needy everywhere he goes. Nathan is a proud military veteran who served in the 82nd Airborne Division as an Airborne Infantry Medic and was able to use that experience, along with his business degree from the University of North Florida, to serve in the medical field for over ten years before moving to Central America full time.

Nathan and his beautiful wife Maria Celeste Pendleton, a native to Nicaragua, have two sons, Isaac and Jeremiah. Nathan and Maria have a special place in their heart for kids with disabilities and special needs — Isaac has cerebral palsy from a traumatic birth. Through this, God is turning what the devil meant for evil into good. It has given them the passion and the vision to start working with the special needs community in Nicaragua, as there is a great need for a physical therapy center and home for orphans with disabilities and terminal illnesses. While Nathan oversees operations, he and Maria continually serve to feed, give fresh water, clothing, new houses, and medical treatment to the poor and needy children and families of Nicaragua.

There are several ways to get involved with the work Deeply Rooted Grounds, *Internationally Registered 501(c)3 Not for Profit* is doing in Nicaragua:

Website: https://www.deeplyrootedgrounds.org/
Instagram: https://www.instagram.com/deeply_rooted_grounds/
Facebook: https://www.facebook.com/deeplyrootedground/
Email: info@deeplyrootedgrounds.org
Phone: +1 (904) 770-6304

You can also connect with Nathan here:

Facebook: https://www.facebook.com/NathanAndrewPendleton
Instagram: https://www.instagram.com/nate_in_nica/
LinkedIn: https://www.linkedin.com/in/nathan-pendleton-700a11182/

CHAPTER 8

Connecting the Dots

Deborah Vick

On the evening of July 15, 2022, I sat stage left, taking a few centering breaths in preparation to enter the stage. I quickly glanced at my cue card, reached down and mindfully stroked my service dog.

A few moments later, I heard the host announce, "Up next is Deborah Vick, Ms. Wheelchair California, USA!"

In my mind, there were a million-and-one things that could go wrong. However, I had already overcome so many other challenges in my life and this event itself, so I was determined to go out and give it my all. Wearing a gorgeous emerald green, off-the-shoulder formal gown and a sparkling tiara, I nervously wheeled up to the microphone and found myself taking a few settling breaths. There we were — my service dog and I — center stage in a pageant, of all places.

I had just begun my timed platform speech, ready to impress the thousands of audience members, celebrity judges, hosts from *People Magazine,* and everyone watching the televised broadcast when I dropped my cue card. I froze in a moment of disbelief, knowing there was no way I could bend down and grab it without exposing more of my top half than the audience had bargained for, yet without that card my cognitive and memory challenges could pose a major problem.

Until a year ago, I never thought of being in any kind of competition, let alone one that includes a beauty component. My dreams and visions of my future have always included some form of public speaking, leadership, community service and legislative advocacy roles. But alongside those dreams, I have also felt many of my lifelong goals and endeavors were sidelined because of my various medical conditions and treatments.

The progressive decline in my health over the years has led me to doubt myself, lose confidence in my identity, lose confidence in my ability to speak and clearly express my message, as well as lose confidence in my appearance. My self-confidence was already limited but kept diminishing as my collection of disorders grew. I have several rare diseases with many common comorbidities: a series of connective tissue disorders including Ehlers-Danlos syndrome, myasthenia gravis and other autoimmune neuromuscular conditions, complex regional pain syndrome (reflex sympathetic dystrophy), and dysautonomia dysfunction, to name a few. I have physical and invisible conditions impacting most joints, muscles, and nerves within my body. Some of the most recent diagnoses have impacted my ability to speak and clearly communicate the thoughts and images within in mind.

When a friend asked me if I would be interested in applying for the pageant leadership role, I had initially thought it was beyond my abilities and comfort level. I was still struggling to find my confidence as a speaker, felt anything but elegant, and would never have envisioned myself as beautiful. However, as uncomfortable as I was, the more I thought about it, the more I realized my message mattered and this platform could help expand my reach. I was already sharing my story as a speaker, mindfulness facilitator and a founder of a nonprofit organization with a vision to empower and engage the disability communities. I realized voicing my experiences had been and continues to be essential, and this includes changing the narrative as to how society looks upon people that appear to be different. It is part of my mission to help young women and men coming of age to feel beautiful in their own skin, to truly love themselves, their whole self.

So, I had decided to step beyond — and I mean way beyond — my comfort level, practically across the entire galaxy, and initiated the application process for the Ms. Wheelchair USA 2022 competition.

Boy, am I glad I did. The growth I experienced through that process was beyond anything I could have imagined. I already knew I have inspired others to step into their own superhero powers by giving a voice to my story, authentically sharing my life's journey, yet I feel I gained so much more than I gave. I not only gained confidence in my voice and in my endeavors, but for the first time in forty-seven years, I can also look in the mirror and see the beauty inside. I can see what so many others have been telling me for a long time. I can see myself for who I truly am.

My ongoing chronic illnesses can lead to a roller coaster ride at any time, and I recently experienced another setback. I am usually pretty good at managing the ups and downs of my varying conditions for some reason, this one hit me a lot harder than previous setbacks. Not only was my physical health posing a significant challenge, but while deciding how to further expand my personal message of empowerment and living my truest purpose, I suddenly faced the oh-so-familiar "I can't" statements and the lurking self-doubt. I thought I had left those limiting beliefs behind six months earlier, a time in which I allowed self-doubt and the fear of "what ifs" to control my mindset. Rather than acknowledging the emotions and continuing to roll forward anyway, for some reason I had gone back to letting these moments control me and hold me back from pursuing my dreams.

Throughout much of my life, I have been a goals-driven individual. The inability to achieve many of my goals has, at times, left me feeling "lesser than." I have grown in leaps and bounds to overcome self-limiting beliefs, but I had never envisioned myself as a pageant participant, beautiful and elegant, wearing crowns and gowns. Quite frankly, I frequently feel like the elephant in a fine porcelain store. (Maybe not the best analogy, as for many people elephants represent "beauty" and "good luck.")

The overall concept of my true vision has, at times, changed over the years, especially with significant changes in life and life-altering medical situations. I recently spoke with several friends who know me quite well, and who have had the opportunity to watch me blossom and discover my own superhero powers. Trustworthy friends can be such a huge help, shining a light on what we might not be seeing in ourselves, and I was truly blown away and honored by their heartfelt sharing. Quite honestly, more than one of these conversations left me in tears of joy and a loss for words.

I have only dared to dream to be able to leave such an impact on the lives of others. Though my path has slightly rerouted to one that practically parallels my original journey, my ultimate vision of empowerment, advocacy, championing equality in education, medical access and legal representation continues to run through my veins. I have such gratitude for having found a "tribe" of amazing people who see greatness in me, support me, believe in me, and compassionately encourage me along my journey.

Initially, I struggled to connect the dots between my vision of empowerment and being a spokeswoman on inclusion, advocacy, and the pageant as a whole. Yes, I know that doesn't quite make sense because the Ms. Wheelchair USA pageant honors women advocates serving our communities in a positive manner and who have some form or forms of mobility impairment. I am choosing to chalk this up to a momentary lapse into "imposter syndrome." Let's be honest with ourselves: most of us have been there at some point or another. I am no exception to the rule.

When I began the application process for Ms. Wheelchair USA and became the state-titled Ms. Wheelchair California, I had a clear set of goals in relation to my platform but had yet to see myself as a successful and empowering spokeswoman. I knew I wanted to leave a legacy of empowerment, inclusion, and teaching people to love and accept themselves for who they are. I felt this was a great way to expand my voice as a speaker and as a nonprofit leader. Beyond that, I did not have grandiose visions. In part because I did not think I would be selected, nor had I envisioned myself in a pageant and speaking on a national stage. My sheer determination to challenge myself and give voice to the experiences of so many others pushed me to pursue this role. A role that was by no means trivial.

This competition is heavily focused on advocacy. Upon acceptance of our state titles, we were expected to attend four or more social- or advocacy-related events every month, centered around our personal advocacy platforms, ones that elevate the overall disability communities, or ones centered around the mission of the Dane Foundation, the parent organization sponsoring the Ms. Wheelchair USA competition. We were expected to post multiple social media posts per week and fundraise for all the entrance fees, hotel, clothing, and other related costs, as the pageant does not cover our costs. We were also expected to fundraise for the Dane Foundation, an organization that helps sponsor the event and creates service-based programs for families with children with developmental disabilities.

At the July 2022 national competition in Ohio, we had events throughout each of the ten days, which was extremely challenging for this body of mine. The last two nights were televised, with a full-set production, opening numbers, interview questions, and delivering two PowerPoint presentations about our respective platforms and marketing strategies while wearing formal evening attire.

I share all this with you since my vision as an advocate, and one who speaks to empowering disadvantaged and underserved communities, has changed throughout this process. As I began to truly embrace the role, new doors opened, and new conversations were sparked. These were opportunities that very likely would not have come my way had I not stepped out of my comfort zone, embraced my fear, and learned to glean all possible lessons from my experience.

It wasn't until the final night, when in some of the worst pain of my life (and that's saying a lot), battling infections, foley bag incidents and challenges with my IV fluids, that I realized all the personal growth I have achieved throughout the year. The power of my voice and my steadfast resolve to shout my story from the valley to the mountain tops started on that stage in that moment.

After dropping my cue card, I took a short, quick breath and scanned the crowd. My eyes connected with my husband, our kids, my parents who had come from Arizona, and my brother who had come from New York. My cousin had also taken the week off work to be with me and help me navigate all aspects of the preparation and competition.

I saw the look of "you've got this" on all their faces, and in that moment I felt my self-confidence switch on. It was the first time I felt as though I truly belonged on that stage, and I didn't need that cue card after all. I quickly settled into my groove as a speaker, mother, wife, daughter, beautiful woman with a disability, and as an advocate, role model and member of a greater community of servant leaders striving to create impactful change locally and abroad. I knew then, as I do now with every ounce of my fiber, my greatness is yet to come.

I'd like to say going from fear to living in my own power was simple, but that would be less than truthful. Learning to turn my pain into my purpose has been a struggle and is an ongoing process. My path is paved with as many successes as there are bumps, pivots and divots. Truth be told, it's a good deal of work. I regularly have to dig deep within myself to connect the dots, remind myself of why it all matters, and find the passion, motivation and determination to continue to push forward, especially during the most challenging days.

If you are anything like me, you might be thinking you do not have a story worth hearing, or others are already sharing journeys similar to yours. This is something I told myself time and time again. However, I chose to continue to push on, as I know my story, experiences, and voice matters. Finding myself in the most unexpected places has allowed me to reach people around the world who connect with my story and my vision. My determination, perseverance, and ability to pivot resonates with a wide range of readers, and my ultimate desire to continue to live my best life while helping others lead their best life inspires me to keep pushing forward against any and all obstacles.

You may be wondering how I transformed the narrative from "I can't" to "I can." In part, this transformational change came through self-empowerment and personal activities that helped my confidence grow. Journaling, using positive "I am" affirmations, and listening to self-help/self-love books and programs may seem a bit cliché, but I promise you these have played a very key role in my pivot from seeing myself as lesser than to seeing myself as the leader, speaker and, yes, the queen that I am today.

There are many masterminds, podcasts and self-help books on mindset, manifestation, and positive affirmations. Many of them have a common thread: we are what we speak into ourselves. As I began to embrace this concept, I learned to create my "I am" statements in terms of how I envision my future self and speaking about my future dreams as if they have already happened. "I am" statements allow me to breathe life into my dreams, manifesting my dreams of tomorrow through my reality today.

My "I am" statements include "I am confident, I am a speaker, I am powerful, I am beautiful, I am strong, and I am a TEDx Speaker." Saying these statements allows me to embrace my abilities in the here and now, as well as those that are yet to be. It is this belief that has allowed me to gain confidence in myself, my voice, and my story, the combination of which has allowed me to step into my power as a speaker, mindfulness facilitator, advocate, and educator.

The change within me was significant and it began my true journey of self-acceptance, self-love and belief in living my true purpose alongside belief in myself. This new perspective has extended into all elements of my life. Finding my voice and my confidence has allowed me to connect in a much deeper way with diverse audiences worldwide. This has led to many more speaking engagements, inclusion in professional programs, training, and invitations to serve on various panels as well as enhancing my current mindfulness practice which includes guided breathwork, mindset, meditation practices, and sound baths.

My speaking presentations frequently center around empowerment, self-confidence, finding my voice, and creating inclusion through what I have named the 3D Effect: Determination, Dynamic Adaptability and Dialogue. I am seeing the story of my journey as one that inspires and motivates others as it has motivated me.

Gaining my confidence and belief in myself is worth its weight in gold. I have connected with global audiences on various platforms in ways which have been unprecedented for me previously. My newly formed abilities have allowed me to see many of my dreams come to fruition and begin turning the gears for those yet to come.

About the Author

Mrs. Deborah Vick is an international speaker, international best-selling author, mindset and leadership facilitator, patient advocate and disABILITY advocate. From an early age Deborah knew it was her desire to be an advocate and spokesperson for people facing injustices, and this desire has inspired her to become the servant leader she is today.

Deborah is a collaborative author in the international best-selling book *Absolute Will*, a contributing author on The Mighty, and is a guest blog writer and contributing author/moderator with Health Union, Inc.'s Myasthenia Gravis's site. She is the founder of a non-profit foundation, and she is dedicated to creating empowering communities for people with disABILITIES and their caregivers while creating the bridge between the business and disability communities. Recently, she was invited to serve on the board of the Peaces of Me Foundation, helping to give a voice to the experiences people with disabilities face in the workforce, academia and in entrepreneurship. Deborah serves as an active community volunteer with activities ranging from Scouting BSA (Boy Scouts of America) to volunteer advocacy with the Christopher and Dana Reeves Foundation, AllStripes, the Myasthenia Gravis Foundation and as Ms. Wheelchair California, USA, 2022. She also serves as an advisory member of the Magical Bridge Foundation, an organization creating inclusive playgrounds for people of all abilities.

Deborah is married to her college sweetheart and is a mother to two loving boys, a service dog, and a recently adopted cat. She has earned her BA in Political Science, M.Ed. in Higher Education with a focus on Diversity Inclusion, and continues to pursue the completion of her law degree. She has completed various continuing education programs, including Mindfulness and Meditation facilitator programs and STEAM programs for elementary schools. Deborah believes that together we can build bridges for a better tomorrow through embracing and embodying the true meaning of the terms "connection, collaboration and community." You can connect with Deborah here:

Website:
https://www.vicktorious.org/

Instagram:
https://www.instagram.com/vicktorious_npo
https://www.instagram.com/forwardrolling/

LinkedIn:
https://www.linkedin.com/in/forwardrolling/

YouTube: https://www.youtube.com/c/DeborahVick

CHAPTER 9

Escaping Two Rocks and a Hard Place

Karlo Dominguez

W*hat is happening to me? I'm only in my mid-thirties. I thought I reached rock bottom one crisis ago, but here I am, at another rock bottom with a lower floor like I'm trying to outdo my previous crisis.*

"Help!" I yelled at the top of my lungs, hoping to wake my sleeping wife. She came running, her face tired from the month of sleepless nights we had both endured because of my restless pain. I had simply been trying to have my morning shower before driving to work, but this time I was stuck. I couldn't lift my leg to get fully into the tub, but also couldn't get back out. How embarrassing.

My wife handed me my phone and I called in sick in the weirdest position possible: clothes off, one leg in the tub and one leg out, as I tried not to fall over because of how weak I'd become. In movies, all the bad things usually happen while in the bathroom.

I did not get to that point overnight, but I suddenly felt as though maybe I should just give up. *I don't want to live anymore. Can I wrap my towel over the shower door and hang myself? It's easy, I'll be pain-free again and free from suffering.* The thoughts consumed my mind for a minute...but then I shook them off and reminded myself, *I'm made of tough stuff. Everyone around me knows it.*

An hour later, we were able to safely get me out of the shower.

I'm a natural introvert. All the things they say about serial killers in true crime documentaries seems to describe me perfectly. I keep to myself, have a small social circle, am socially awkward, quiet, smart, meticulous, and I pay close attention to tiny details. I also enjoy going outside my home, though, if it's to catch a good movie at the nearby theater or eat at restaurants to try unique dishes. I'm not one to just sit around wasting time. I play hard but I work hard too. In fact, I'm a workaholic. Despite being introverted, I have a way of speaking in a relatable manner. Combining that natural ability with my work ethic, I have reached positions answering to executives in my company. Life was good, and I was dreaming of being a company director one day.

That's when the gateway to my first crisis hit: my wife suffered a miscarriage in January 2021. The news hit me hard; I felt like I was sleepwalking. This was supposed to be our first child. A month prior, it had been the perfect holiday miracle to learn she was pregnant. I was so excited, and curious as to what kind of father I would be. I cried for an entire day and then it was as though all the lights inside me turned off, one by one.

I turned off as a person.
I turned off wanting to achieve my vision of becoming a director.

I especially turned off being a good husband to my wife. Our marriage was suffering, and I put it on the rocks intentionally. The sins I committed while I was turned off run deep and are unforgivable. My wife had every right to want to leave me, and I didn't think we would make it to the end of 2021.

In June 2021, I quit my job. I was still struggling emotionally, and my egotistical reaction came after hearing a new company would be taking over and they planned to decrease my salary. My ego still had me convinced I would be a director someday, and this felt like my big chance to gamble on finding a better position elsewhere. My expectation was not reality.

Despite it all, good people guided us through this crisis with prayers, words of advice, and counseling, and we survived. Without their help, I would not have been able to flip the switch on again and get back on track to take care of the things that truly matter in my life. I would not have been able to learn how to forgive myself and allow myself to have greater emotions. I started thinking I don't need to be a director of anything. If I had trouble controlling my life, then I would have trouble controlling a whole department of people!

As soon as things started to settle down and realign back to normal at home, I started to feel some pain in my heels. This was the start of my second rock bottom.

My pains started in August 2021, a few weeks after my first crisis subsided. I had just started a new job which wasn't the director role I hoped for, but I had bills to pay, and this job would do for the time being.

I told myself, *I must have sciatica again.* Gradually, my mobility declined. I couldn't go up and down any stairs at work without pain, and eventually I could not even get up one step. My walking speed went to a crawl. Standing up from a low chair was extremely difficult and my hips would always pop. My knees were aching all the time. I couldn't even dress myself without my wife's help. I was in denial and thinking I would just "work through it" and get my job done.

My ego spoke to me many times as I continued to collect new lows.

How humiliating. You pride yourself in what you can get done with your own hands, now you can't even get your foot into a pant leg by yourself or put on your own socks. Are you embarrassed yet? You didn't make it to the bathroom today because you couldn't get up from your chair. There are three-year-olds with better control of their bladder than you.

Then one day at work, around mid-October, my office chair rolled away from me when I stood up for a break. Halfway to my standing position, my legs just gave out. I yelled some words I can't write here and the next thing I knew...BOOM! I was on my back looking up at the lights overhead.

My coworkers rushed to help me, some asking if I was okay and some frozen in disbelief at what they had just witnessed. I got up on my own from a mix of sheer embarrassment and adrenaline, quickly grabbed all my things and left for the day. Sitting in my car outside the office building, I thought, *I have to do something, I need to know what's wrong,* so I called my doctor. He informed me it would be a four-month wait to see a specialist.

A couple of weeks later, there I was in my birthday suit, one leg in the shower and one leg out, on the phone telling my boss I wouldn't be coming to work.

By Christmas I was on disability leave, after many urgent care and emergency-room visits, trying all kinds of pain-relief products including a $500 CBD cream, and even buying a new SUV because I couldn't get in or out of my other car. I was walking with a cane to get around regularly during the day. At night, I was sleeping on my recliner couch because of how much it would hurt to get out of bed. I also started getting severely itchy skin. My head was so cut up by my scratching you can still see the patterns of scars through my hair.

I was in pain, unemployed, and relying on my wife's job income. What a stark contrast to the excitement I'd felt just one year before. Life didn't look anything like I'd thought it would. Tough times were in store, but I had to think positively. I reassured myself that at least we had enough money saved to weather this storm. Call it an affirmation, a lie, or wishful thinking, it was necessary to start thinking positively or else I would never make it to the opposite end of wherever this was leading me.

A week after New Year's Day, a dermatologist diagnosed me with psoriasis during my checkup and said my pains were most likely psoriatic arthritis, which can precede the skin issues. I finally knew what was wrong with me. By February 2022, that diagnosis was confirmed too: I had psoriatic arthritis affecting every joint, from my shoulders to my feet. By that point, I was at my weakest; using a walker to get around. A slight breeze was able to knock me over, but being stubborn, I wanted to be able to do one thing that I used as a test against my condition. I needed to maintain some sense of control of my life, and not let what I was feeling take away from who I am, so I managed to force myself to continue driving, although just for short distances.

Some days I mourned how I used to get around without a walker or cane. I was angry about what I had lost and what I had become, and realized I had to make another choice: *Do I stay angry and let it defeat me, or do I learn to live with what I have then challenge myself to do a little more each day?*

The easy thing would have been to just quit fighting and be defeated. I could have let my health condition consume me and let everyone pity me. *I turned off once, do I turn off again? No.*

Instead, I chose to learn to adapt to what pains I felt day to day. I decided it was time to learn how to live with this and let it guide me in doing things that did not put me in pain or that didn't hurt too much, rather than letting it consume me as an excuse to do nothing with my life.

After making that decision, I started to tackle simple chores around the house based on what I could and couldn't do. *That's too heavy, I can't lift it. I can wash dishes, though.* Next was reaching into the fridge to feed myself again. *That's too low, I can't reach it.* My wife rearranged the fridge so I could reach for things to snack on. *I can feed myself.* When I wanted to fry chicken and realized the pot was too heavy, my wife moved some pots and pans to the stovetop so I didn't have to worry about dropping things. *I can feed us both again.*

After being put on a bi-weekly injection regimen, I was finally on a path to healing and could see a light at the end of the tunnel. Three months later, I went from walking with a walker to walking with a cane again. My skin and scalp were getting better as well. Day by day, I continued improving, and my small wins got bigger and bigger.

It was not an easy road, but my simple wins drove me to get back the life I thought I'd lost. As I gradually healed, I was able to do more than before. Winning small helped me regain my confidence because the next challenge was always asking a little bit more from myself than the last. I could see the light, but I was still only halfway through the tunnel. My disability benefits ran out in April, and by June I had to leave the company because they wanted me to pay my benefits out of pocket. That would have financially ruined us. Remember how I lied to myself early on that we would survive on savings? We were running out of money, so the next task was going to be a big one: getting back to work.

We managed to make it through by cutting back on excessive and compulsive spending, and thankfully I was hired into a new job a few months later. Today I'm living as close to a "normal" life as possible, which for me feels extraordinary. Yes, the vision I had for my life has changed along the way, and yes, I still have pain and symptoms that may never completely go away, but I do not let these things defeat me. I was truly humbled by my crises.

Part of me still wants to be a director, but I know it's my ego wanting that, not the real me. The things I truly want for myself and my life are peace of mind, peace of heart, and to live as free as I define it. I was able to change my mind and escape from being wedged between two rocks and a hard place. I found my way by more clearly expressing my emotions and allowing myself to feel my feelings. My stubbornness and perseverance to achieve even the smallest wins eventually helped me win big.

I don't know where you may be in your life and what rocks are weighing you down. Maybe you're in a weird position like I was at the beginning, stuck, with one foot in and one foot out. I want to challenge you to be stubborn, don't give up, and lie to yourself when you need to — these actions will determine your success. Positive statements, even half-truths at first, will result in positive outcomes. Your wins may seem small at first, but they will build on each other. Just taking one step often motivates us to take a few more.

I would not be where I am today without my faith in God, my faith in myself, my closest friends, and without the support of my loving wife. Having a support system will be key to getting through the journey you are on for the great visions you have in life. When you doubt yourself, those are the people who will remind you of what you are capable of and put you back on the path to reaching your goals.

I've grown as a person because of what I've been through. I'm at the end of the tunnel now looking back at how far I've walked through the darkness. I know my path has many more dark tunnels that I haven't reached yet, and when I do, I'm confident I will be able to get through them as well with my strength, stubbornness, and perseverance.

About the Author

Karlo Dominguez is a United States Navy veteran who is currently a cybersecurity professional employed by a major credit scoring company. This is his first time authoring a chapter, and he is considering writing a book of his own in the future. He currently lives in Hawaii on the island of Oahu with his wife, Emelryn Vebs Dominguez, and two cockatiels, Sunny and Luna. They have just purchased a new home, and it has already kept them extremely busy.

When he is not moonlighting as an author, Karlo enjoys reading fictional books, absorbing movies and TV, talking to himself, winning old arguments in his mind, and trying to keep up with current slang through online gaming. Karlo also enjoys heavy sarcasm, humor of all forms, memes, and is a sucker for a good crab cake and fried calamari.

Karlo loves traveling and has been to Spain, Japan, Canada, Philippines, and numerous states throughout the US. His latest adventure was

Fairbanks, Alaska, where he had a life-defining encounter after seeing the Aurora Borealis up close and personal.

If you want to connect with Karlo, you can follow him on LinkedIn: https://www.linkedin.com/in/karlo-d-b6254136/

Please feel free to email him with your praise, comments, concerns, one-liners, secret family recipes, and memes.

Email: karlodominguez@tutanota.com

CHAPTER 10

A Different Spin

Lindsay Malkinson

Tears filled my eyes. *Is this really what life is supposed to be like? Is this the plan?* My heart broke when I heard my diagnosis. I just couldn't believe this was going to be my life.

My mom had gone through a difficult pregnancy with me. She bled from 7-17 weeks, had an amniotic fluid loss at 20 weeks and had to be on bed rest from 20-30 weeks. She was sick with influenza during those 10 weeks of bed rest and had a fever for a few days. At 39 weeks, labor was induced. My mom has told me I was a beautiful baby with lots of dark hair, I breastfed like a champ, and I didn't cry very much.

As a toddler, I walked and talked late; I didn't start walking until I was nineteen months old. I live in my own little world. I am not blind, but I see things differently. I am not deaf, but I hear things differently. I am not trapped, but it is hard for me to feel free. I don't think the same way as neurotypical people. My thoughts are abstract.

My parents had noticed there was something going on with me; that there were certain "age-appropriate" things I could and couldn't do. By the time I was eleven years old, in Grade 6, I had already been on several medications for two years, been to many years' worth of medical appointments, and life had been getting more and more difficult with the passing of time. After a couple of misdiagnoses, my parents decided to get me assessed at the BC Children's hospital in Vancouver, British Columbia, Canada.

Autism.

Had I been diagnosed sooner, I feel it would have been easier for my family and me to understand the multiple challenges I faced growing up. We could have dealt with my challenges in a different way. Autism is not a disability; it's a different ability and a different way of learning. I believe the reason I have autism is that my nervous system did not develop properly, but genetics could also have played a role. What I experienced before my diagnosis and since has caused me anxiety, and the things I have found most helpful are music, noise-canceling headphones, weighted blankets and distracting myself with activity books such as Sudoku and word searches.

For me, the hardest part about life on the spectrum is communication. When I was younger, I struggled because I often couldn't get my words out, which was frustrating and upsetting. My family and I didn't really see eye to eye as I was growing up. I'm an emotional person, and I care deeply about other people, which makes me vulnerable. I feel my feelings deeply, and when I find a friend I care about, I've been told I seem to care too much. It's been very difficult for me to make and keep friends.

My home was my safe place to get my frustrations out, and in school and other social settings my difficulty communicating led me to isolate myself as a way of coping. I didn't fit in, I felt out of place, and I didn't understand why I was the way I was. Autism makes me feel like there is a clear glass wall I can see through, but I can't get to the other side.

I have been bullied, taken advantage of, and told things no one ever wants to hear. I was heartbroken when I was told by medical professionals that I was behind, that I'd reach milestones more slowly than my peers and my chances of succeeding would be lower. It made me determined to prove everyone wrong.

Despite being told to quit French class because it would be too much of a workload, my parents fought to keep me in the academic program, and I graduated in 2017 with a Grade 12 certificate. Every year I qualified for the honor and merit rolls, I achieved the top Grade 10 science award in the entire school, I earned Grade 12 psychology and food awards, and I even won two scholarships. I'm smart, I have excellent attention to detail, I am a talented photographer, and when I set my mind towards goals, I accomplish them.

To this day I still struggle with my balance, so I am proud of myself for learning to figure skate. Honestly, I could have given up because I was so frustrated. Seeing others advance quicker than me was disappointing, but I made the choice to put a different spin on it: even though I don't succeed as fast as my peers, it's up to me whether I take these challenges as failures or as opportunities for growth. Life isn't a competition or a race, and we all excel at our own pace. I now strongly believe I can do anything I set my mind to because I've proven it to myself. When people told me I wouldn't succeed as fast, it made me think about my future in a new way. I decided I had to create my own vision for my life. Autism has taught me to celebrate every victory, even the little ones, and I am very proud of how far I've come.

Autism falls on a wide-range spectrum, and has been around for many years, but has been underdiagnosed. I am surprised, but some people on the spectrum prefer to be called autistic. I personally do not like that term because I like to be addressed as an individual, not identified by my diagnosis, but everyone on the spectrum has different preferences. I prefer to be called *a person with autism*. We are all unique, with different traits, like a snowflake. So many amazing people are known to be or have been on the spectrum: Albert Einstein, Bill Gates, and Temple Grandin to name a few. Being on the autism spectrum is just another way of comprehending the world; another way of processing what I'm experiencing around me.

I was very nervous to share in the beginning, because of how badly I have been treated. I used to not want people to know I had it and I would break down and cry when people talked about my autism; I was afraid of being judged, afraid of people thinking I was weird. It was scary at first knowing this is something I will have forever, but I now know how to make the best of my diagnosis.

I feel like my calling is to educate about life with autism and to inspire and empower others. I am proud of how far I have come despite the challenges I have faced, and I am grateful for a lot of things in my life. I now run my own business. I've realized I could either pout about my situation or make the best of it. I changed my mindset from "poor me" to using my story as an opportunity to inspire others. I had to pivot the way I looked at the world and I decided I can either take what is thrown at me as a disappointment or an opportunity to inspire others. I've realized that each day we wake up is an opportunity for growth that many people don't get to experience. So instead of complaining about what I don't have or what I wish my life wasn't, I see my diagnosis as an opportunity for my growth, I appreciate what I do have and what I am making of my life with autism. I value the little things and try to enjoy every moment because we never know when it might be our last.

Looking around me, I've discovered that everyone is going through a battle of some sort, and knowing this about others can give us all an opportunity to make connections despite our differences. Everyone goes through struggles, so always be kind and you will always be right. Treat people the way you want to be treated; it's that simple. I want the world to see that though there is pain and suffering, there are still good people — and I want to make the world a better place by giving back to the less fortunate, taking time to listen and learn, and being a voice for those who can't speak for themselves.

My view on my autism diagnosis has changed over the years. In the beginning, I wished I didn't have autism. My anxiety held me back from talking about it or feeling like I could be inspirational. I wished I didn't feel like things were always my fault. I've always said if I could change one thing, it would be for me not to have autism and anxiety, but now I'm proud to be on the autism spectrum.

I may be different, but I'm not less than anybody else. I had a lot of hopes and dreams when I was younger about how my life would turn out. I wondered how old I would be when I became a homeowner, or what it would be like to have a family. The vision I had for my life and my future isn't what I thought it would be, but I've learned that even when life doesn't turn out the way we had planned, this can still be a good thing.

That's not to say life on the autism spectrum is easy. It isn't. Knowing I will have to live on the spectrum for the rest of my life was difficult to accept at first, but now I'm grateful I get to be a beacon of light for others. Everybody is in this world for a reason, and even when we cannot see, we can still be an inspiration for those around us.

* * *

My younger sister Erin wrote this poem for a 4H presentation when she was thirteen years old. Autism is a topic she enjoys learning about and I'm so proud of her.

Don't Fear Her, It's Just Autism —
by Erin Malkinson, shared with her permission.

I know what a lot of you think when you hear the word autism,
But whatever you think is wrong unless it's right.
When I hear that complex idea of a word,
I think they must be really overlooked,
Because they are.

My sister has autism.
It has been hard for her and my whole family.
She feels like our parents are shoving her in the darkness.

She wants to claw out,
But what she doesn't know is they're trying to lead her into the
sunlight, where her smile of hope and joy can shine bright.

She's underestimated, unappreciated, unapproachable to some,
But if you didn't know she had it, you wouldn't be able to tell.

You wouldn't know her heart is as pure as gold.
If only you would stop to learn,
The autism isn't her, it's only part of her.
So don't fear her, it's just autism.

About the Author

Lindsay Malkinson lives in British Columbia, Canada, and is a dog mom to a Shih Tzu Papillon named Panda. Lindsay is proud to say she is a Grade 12 graduate (since 2017) with a Dogwood certificate.

Lindsay was diagnosed with autism and anxiety when she was in Grade 6, and this diagnosis led her to make holistic changes that include using pure essential oils and creating a toxin-free lifestyle.

Lindsay runs a Young Living business and loves helping others by offering solutions to support their health and wellness needs. Because of her experience and perspective, she specifically enjoys working with and inspiring young adults and women on the spectrum.

Lindsay's astrology sign is Cancer, she has always been fascinated with the sky, her favorite holiday is Christmas, and some of her hobbies include photography, listening to music, watching *Dancing with the Stars*, and spending time with her family and friends who mean a lot to her.

This is Lindsay's first book collaboration, and even if you don't have autism, she hopes from reading her story it inspires you and helps you to know you aren't alone.

You can connect with Lindsay here:

Instagram:
https://www.instagram.com/inspiringessentials/

Facebook Groups:
https://www.facebook.com/groups/aroundlife
https://www.facebook.com/groups/inspiringessentials

Email: lindsay.malkinson@gmail.com

CHAPTER 11

The Broken Link

Rosa Lopez Silva

I f we don't experience the chill of a dark winter, we would not be able to cherish the warmth of a bright summer. Nothing stimulates our appetite for victory more than starvation caused by traumatic events.

As a kid, I dreamed of being a lawyer. I remember pulling out an old suitcase my parents had in a closet, putting textbooks in it, and wearing my nice pair of blue dress pants and a white-collar shirt as I pretended to walk to the court. My dad used to tell me nothing was impossible to accomplish if I put the idea in my mind and took action.

But having dysfunctional, alcoholic parents, made me give up on my dream and instead the door opened to my living hell of events. When I was eleven years old, my parents divorced, our family split up, and because the cartels were killing innocent people and destroying everything in their way, my mother migrated with me, my sister and my brother from Michoacan, Mexico, to the United States. My dad stayed behind, and it was the last time I ever saw him.

My mother enrolled us in school in the United States, which I was grateful for. It's a privilege kids don't often get in Mexico. But despite the excitement of being able to go to school, my emotions were a mess; my daily home life was in upheaval, and I missed my dad and my country. My mom was drinking, bringing home many different men, and eventually one of them raped me and my sister. As horrendous as that experience was, it wasn't even the most painful part: when we confided in our mom what had happened, she kicked us out of our home and kept him instead. We were just kids, sixteen and seventeen, but our childhood was suddenly ripped from us.

The pain, self-disgust, depression, and anger dragged me into a deep, black hole. According to my disturbed mind, drugs and alcohol helped me cope, but they, in reality, are silent killers, chasing you every night, coming to take your life away.

Alcoholism is very common, and since many go through it we think it is normal when it is not. It is a sickness and destroys everything in and around you. The same way it destroyed my parents, it destroyed me. I became pregnant at seventeen years old. I was homeless and stopped taking care of myself. I couldn't stop using substances and drinking while I was pregnant — my body needed them. I tried quitting on my own, but the side effects of not using were impossible to handle. I was afraid of losing my baby to Child Protective Services when it was time to give birth, but God's protection was upon us.

Alcohol and drugs were what helped me bear the emotional and mental pain I was going through. My life was dark, I missed my family, and I felt more and more empty inside. I kept hearing about how no one wanted to be around me because I was an alcoholic, but no one offered to help. My veins were always black and popped from shooting heroin into them. My nostrils bled constantly from the heavy amounts of cocaine I used. I remember telling myself, *I know one day soon I'll die. My kidneys and liver will just give up on me.*

Though I knew the risks, I couldn't stop; I didn't know how to stop. The emotional anguish kept on taking me deeper and deeper. After having my daughter, I tried to work but lost several jobs due to my alcoholism. It was impossible for me to stay sober. I lost weight and stopped keeping myself clean. My teeth looked nasty, as did my skin. I was always in a bad mood and carried on a love-hate relationship with drugs and alcohol. Some days my daughter and I were able to stay with people I knew, but no one offered me a permanent home, which was understandable because of my addiction.

Eventually, I married an older man thinking that would be my salvation. I felt very fortunate that he wanted to marry me and give my daughter and me a place to call home, but it was just another painful time in my life: for the next two years I had to live with his verbal and sexual abuse. While going through domestic abuse, I was able to stop using drugs, but not alcohol, as he was a heavy drinker too. Who you surround yourself with has a lot to do with being able to quit or continue an addiction.

When a California highway patrol officer called me one day to let me know my mom had been in a very bad car accident, that was my wake-up call. She had been driving while heavily intoxicated, with my three younger brothers in the car. The oldest one almost died. By then I was a mom of two and I suddenly realized my life was heading for the same outcome as hers, or worse. When she went to prison, she lost custody of my siblings, who were sixteen, nine and eight years old, and they were given to me. I became a mom of five in a blink of an eye while trying to cope with domestic abuse, and it was enough to turn me to drugs again.

The more I struggled with my addictions and the stress of my situation, the more I realized I had unintentionally started hurting my kids and had not realized all the emotional damage I had done. Too many tragic stories had been repeated for too many years throughout my past generations. Looking into my daughter's crying eyes, I knew exactly how she felt at seeing me falling to pieces, drunk, and dirty. I had once been that little girl, crying while my parents destroyed each other through their alcoholism and physical violence.

I had lost everything and everyone I loved, my dad had died from colon cancer, my mom was in jail, my own kids were suffering, my brothers were struggling with depression, I was a drinker again, and had given up on my dreams.

I was tired of being tired. I realized where I had ended up was because of one wrong decision after another, starting with my parents and now I was doing the same to my kids. I reminded myself I had once been an A+ student who migrated from Mexico, and I knew I could do better. I had successfully overcome so many challenges back then, so I knew I could do it again. My kids became my focus, my drive, and my strength to face everything ahead of us.

My own family was going to have a different story. My baby daughter gave me the strength to move forward, get professional help, and detox myself.

Traumatic events are like a chain, and we are the only ones able to break them apart. Many times, hearing abusive words once said to me would put me right back into victim mode, blind to reality and ignoring my own power. Turning my life around after so many years of emotional, physical, and mental turmoil was no easy task. The struggle was real.

It took the love of my daughter's grandparents to help me out of this darkness. They provided what I needed to seek professional help and helped me get a car so that I could start working again. That car was a blessing because it was also the vehicle I used to flee my abusive relationship. I ran away so I could start a new life.

There were days when anxiety was hard to deal with, but I knew I had to take things one day at a time. I did meditation and got serious about creating a dream board with pictures. My therapist helped me discover holding on to past pain was the cause of becoming an addict and alcoholic, and my move away from the people that provided the drugs and alcohol allowed me to have a fresh start. When you are an addict, many people are there to help keep you addicted but few are there to help you get sober. For me it was none. I had to save myself.

I began to pick up all the broken pieces and put myself back together. In 2007, I moved from southern California to a small town called Fairfield in northern California. My older brother got accepted at Berkeley University, I met my now husband, had two more babies, had the wedding of my dreams on a private yacht, graduated high school in 2021, started my own beauty business, purchased my first home in Florida, where I reside now, invested in my first food trailer, traveled all over the United States, became a makeup artist, and learned to have a healthy relationship with alcohol and myself. I did not become a lawyer as I had dreamed of as a kid, but I am an entrepreneur. I still wear my blue pants and my white shirt to remind myself to never let anything take my happiness and dreams away again.

Now I have a beautiful family, a better understanding of myself, a clear vision of what I want, where I'm going, and I finally understand that I needed to go through the darkness to learn how to paint a beautiful rainbow after a storm.

Somehow my first child made it through my suicidal attempts, drugs, and alcohol. She is the most valuable gift that I once felt I didn't deserve, but now she is my biggest reminder of how strong I became. There is no going back to that dark life.

Now I am dedicated to giving back to my community by helping other women escape the grip of their addictions and start taking steps to recovery. Through my beauty business I have met many women who felt ugly, and a makeover made them discover how beautiful they really are, inside and out.

I love taking pictures for my social media, sharing inspiration, and I love connecting with and encouraging other women to pursue their dreams too. One of my next big visions is to open a homeless shelter and a domestic abuse center.

It only took someone with human kindness to help me turn my life around, and I know I can pay it forward to be the little ray of light to other women going through the same situation as me. I envision women united, empowering others to live a better life for themselves and their kids, being able to live an abundant life of happiness and peace, teaching them to discover that though we may give up on a dream at times, we are equipped with many talents that can lead to a successful career. I also want to teach women the signs and feelings on every stage of addiction and detox so that they can be brave to take the next step to rehabilitation through my woman revelation center.

I wouldn't be able to do this without having gone through my journey. Our scars can be a blessing to others, to help them realize they are not alone in their struggles. I was once blind to that aspect of what I went through, but now I see life through different lenses. I can't change my past, but the choices I make today can make my tomorrow very different. I opened my mind, got out of my comfort zone, and decided I no longer wanted to be in a downward spiral. One of my biggest mistakes in life was serving everyone else first and ignoring my own needs. We can't serve and take care of others if we are not okay. I learned to love myself, and to make myself a priority.

We need to take time to cry and heal, but it's not healthy to get stuck there. The past is the past. It's important to find ways to look forward to tomorrow and to continue moving in the direction you want your life to go. Even when there are things we can't change after we think we've tried everything, let it go and have faith it will work out as it should.

The hardest part of turning my life around was asking for forgiveness from others and forgiving people who have caused me pain. I also had to forgive myself. I am not in a position to judge, and I realized holding grudges and resentment was not going to give me my freedom. I had repeated a lot of the mistakes my parents made. I had abused my kids in many ways with my actions. I had to pay my dues and decided that we were breaking those chains together like the united family we are.

The broken link is what changed my kids' future. I made the decision that my kids' lives will be different, and I am the only one who can make it happen. I am very grateful they have forgiven me, and that life gave us a second chance. Day by day our hearts are healing, and we are learning how to be stronger together.

Traumatic events can turn out to be a blessing, though we can't see that while going through them. When we are faced with challenges, they can seem scary or even dangerous, but when we finally drive through the storm and reach the other side, the view is beautiful and worth admiring. Let life be the beautiful rainbow it can be. Do not allow anyone or anything in life to take that away from you. And don't give up on your dreams.

Alcoholism and drug addiction are curable if we seek help and stand strong. Fight the good fight, and never forget how valuable you are. You are a ray of hope to your little ones and to many others around you.

Being raped, being mentally abused by my alcoholic parents, attempting to commit suicide, becoming a drug addict and alcoholic, experiencing domestic violence and family losses, almost caused me to disappear into the darkness. But instead, I've chosen to create a life of colorful rainbows and to look for the beauty after the storm.

About the Author

Rosa Lopez Silva is from Michoacan, Mexico and lives in Florida, United States. She is married to Edwin Lopez from El Salvador, and their "army" is made of his, hers, and their kids: Delilah is 22, Abby 20, Anthony 18, Abel 14, and Darlene 11. The family also has four cats: Lori, Dusk, Pelitos, and Rainy.

Rosa is a high-school graduate, currently works part-time as an administrative assistant in a successful construction company and has become an entrepreneur. She is also a professional makeup artist and skincare consultant, trains women to be independent sales representatives, and she has recently started a food trailer chain. She loves developing businesses to create multiple sources of income.

Rosa loves traveling, meeting people, trying different cultures' foods, watching sunsets and sunrises, listening to music, investing, going to the beach, and helping others in need. In her free time, she loves doing makeovers to help women see their beauty inside and out. Rosa also enjoys participating in various fundraisers; these kinds of events have helped her meet people all over the world who support and help make dreams come true for those in need.

One of her goals is to teach her kids to fill their hearts with love and give back to anyone in need in the world. It only takes one person's love to change someone else's darkness. Rosa recently started mentoring women to be financially independent and to pursue owning their own businesses without a college degree, and to create a legacy they can pass on to their kids.

Rosa's mission is to show other women the road to freedom and self-love, walking away from darkness and self-destruction.

Connect with Rosa here:

Website:
https://www.jafra.com/wingswest

Instagram:
https://www.instagram.com/wingswest01/

WhatsApp: (863) 517-8955

Email: wingswestllc@gmail.com

CHAPTER 12

Under a Palm Tree

Mike Boone

I t felt like being in kindergarten again. We'd been invited to a New Year's Eve party with a purpose, and the invite came with instructions: "Bring a stack of magazines and a big piece of Bristol board."

Our friend Angela called it a vision-board party. My then-girlfriend Jo and I thought it was an odd idea for a New Year's gathering to have people drinking and using scissors, but Ang and her then-husband Cory were good friends of ours, and we didn't want to be difficult.

We were told to find pictures, words, or phrases in the magazines that would remind us daily of the dreams and goals we wanted for our future. Jo and I were both in the middle of lengthy, stressful, expensive legal battles with our ex-spouses. We were barely making ends meet. Jo's health was failing. We felt frustrated and stuck in continual fight mode because of court proceedings every few months. We desperately wanted to put our roller coaster past behind us and start our new lives with our vision for the future.

We drank and cut up magazines all evening while gluing the images to our board. We even printed out a picture of the Caribbean we found online. We dreamed as big as we could, laughing at the impossibility of it all, saying over and over, "Could you imagine?"

It was fun to pretend, but the images on our board could never *really* happen. As far as I was concerned, this was just a reason to drink with our friends.

As 2016 started, Jo and I each went back to the daily grind of my job as a septic truck driver, our divorce dramas, doctor visits and lots of missed work for Jo because of lupus and other autoimmune diseases she had, waking up every morning and looking at the vision board we created, and just wanting life to be better.

A month later, my ninety-one-year-old grandmother passed away. Nan was the family rock; happy, generous, and always helping others throughout her life. When my parents divorced in 1983, I was only eight years old, and for the following two years, Nan gave me and my older brother a safe, loving place to live while their ugly battle ensued. After my mum had made the difficult choice to end their marriage and leave me and my ten-year-old brother behind, my father's anger and hate boiled over. He did everything he could to prevent my mum from talking to us or visiting us, and he eventually destroyed our family home. Through all the violence and craziness, my nan was always there for us, always willing to listen and inspire. Even at such a young age, I tried to forget the bad and stay as positive as I could, and I still remember my nan and I cooking in her kitchen when I told her, "One day I'll have a restaurant under a palm tree." She never let me forget that.

Life's challenges kept coming: my father's wild party years ended abruptly when he married one of my high school teachers and they had two sons together. It was a difficult new family dynamic with babies in the house, and at age sixteen I moved out, dropped out of high school, and got a full-time job cooking. After my girlfriend graduated, we headed west. Three months later we had a baby of our own on the way and moved back to our hometown of Dryden, Ontario. By age 23, I was married with two daughters, and the financial strain was taking its toll. I needed to improve our situation, so we moved west again. Out of four restaurants I worked for, two closed seasonally, one went bankrupt, and one burned down shortly after we made the front page of the newspaper for a Christmas dinner gone wrong. With such a disappointing track record, I gave up cooking, bought a taxi and hired a driver, only to have him sink it in the city drinking reservoir, making the front page of the paper yet again.

You're probably wondering why I didn't give up at that point, but with family responsibilities, that just wasn't an option. I decided to get my commercial driver's license, something my father always compared to a college degree. But it had its challenges as well. Logging in the mountains of British Columbia, Canada, was one of the most dangerous jobs I ever had, and over the years I ended up rolling three trucks, once closing the highway for nine hours and making the front page of the newspaper for the third time. Log truck driving was my father's occupation and was my connection to feeling acceptance from him. He's been hard on me my whole life. I was never good enough, could never do anything right, and was always treated differently than my three brothers. Even though as an adult now I have come to understand him more, it hasn't made it any easier to still be the son who triggers his anger.

I had financed my own Peterbilt and was transporting materials all over North America until the global financial crisis in 2008 brought everything to a screeching halt. After the bank repossessed my transport and foreclosed on our house, it wasn't long before my marriage started to fall apart, eventually ending in a lengthy, expensive divorce.

I've always used music to help me through hard times. It's something my father shared with us as kids and, as difficult as our relationship has been, I'm grateful he instilled his appreciation of music in me. I have a song list I try to listen to every day to get me through troubled times and motivate me to keep moving forward with a positive mindset. One of my favorites is "Closing Time" by Semisonic, which came out around the time the last bar I worked at burned down. The song resonates with so many aspects of my life, my career in hospitality, great memories with my mum throughout her career in hospitality, and the lyrics: "Every new beginning comes from some other beginning's end."

So with my nan's passing in January 2016, I felt like she reached out by leaving me a bit of money, knowing I would use it for something fun. I googled "vacations on a budget," and from a list of ten affordable countries, Nicaragua was number seven. Jo and I decided to spend a week on the Corn Islands, two remote islands off Nicaragua's east coast, in the Caribbean. As our plans came together and as we got more excited, Jo's two-year divorce finally wrapped up, giving us some relief. Mine, on the other hand, wouldn't be finalized for another three years.

We both knew someday we wanted to live somewhere tropical, and the Caribbean was one of the first things we had put on our vision board only a month earlier. We decided to keep open minds on our vacation and consider if we could see ourselves ever actually doing it. Falling in love with Nicaragua was easy; Big Corn Island was paradise. We started talking real estate the moment we landed, and within a day or two we met a Canadian expat who happened to be selling land.

This wasn't a cute, manicured yard. We couldn't just drive by to see it. We're talking acres and acres of jungle vines and bushes so thick we had to have a local islander chop a trail for us with a huge machete as we walked up the hill to figure out what we were even looking at.

Part of the land had remains of the island's historic rock wall, built by the first islanders in the 1700s. Along with the typical Caribbean folklore of pirates and buried treasures, the history of the rock wall was intriguing. Jo had a hard time seeing the potential I saw, but I knew this was the beginning of our Caribbean vision. I felt it. I wanted it. I even knew where I wanted to build my restaurant.

We only needed a couple of days to decide to buy two acres, and when we got back to Canada we set our plan in motion by downsizing and selling everything we wouldn't be taking with us. Jo had two condominiums, so we lived in one while renovating it and then sold both. We packed up our Durango and cargo trailer with all we had left, and in early December 2016 we started the nearly 6,000-mile drive from Vancouver Island, British Columbia to Big Corn Island, Nicaragua, thinking we might never come back.

Several countries we had to cross on the way were known as dangerous for travelers. Here I was, a guy with dreadlocks, my girlfriend, my dog, in an SUV towing a cargo trailer full of everything we owned, heading for Central America. What could go wrong?

As a trucker, I'm used to driving long distances and navigating cities I've never been to before. But running out of fuel at night on a snowy mountain pass in Texas was the start of many obstacles to come. The entire trip was eventful, somewhat frustrating at times, and as Jo will tell anyone who asks, had a few occasions when she was pretty sure we were going to be killed. In Mexico we got stopped at a highway roadblock where guys were holding giant machetes and asking for money. One thing I was taught by my nan is to have trust in everyone until they show you they can't be trusted. After some tense moments, and Jo using the translate app on her phone as I tried to scare them away by showing them our big dog, it turned out the roadblock warriors just wanted 60 pesos (US$3) to be used for school upgrades. *No problema.*

Crossing into Guatemala was much more expensive. Border agents told us to pay US$800 as a tax on our vehicle and belongings, and when Jo argued, they locked our SUV and trailer behind the iron gates to what looked like a chop shop. We were stranded overnight until we paid the tax the following morning to get on our way. Otherwise, we wouldn't have been allowed to enter Guatemala, and turning back was not an option.

The daytime drive across El Salvador and along the coastline was absolutely breathtaking, but driving the treacherous Honduras roads at night and going through multiple military checkpoints was nerve-racking. By the time we arrived in Nicaragua, we were ready for no more drama. We drove east across the country and then boarded the Captain

D ship for an eighteen-hour journey through the winding Rama River and out into the open ocean to Big Corn Island.

Things on the island were more expensive than we budgeted for, and construction of our first building took longer than I had hoped. We flew back to Vancouver Island only eight months later, completely broke, with nowhere to live, two suitcases in hand, and everything else left behind in Nicaragua. It was deflating. We had plans for several rental units and of course my restaurant, but the first house was only half-built. It was such a disappointment to have been so close and then feel like we were starting over.

We realized rebuilding our finances needed to be a priority, so in 2018 we moved back to northwestern Ontario to relieve a lot of the financial burden of life on the expensive west coast. Even though building our Caribbean dream has had even more challenges since, we are now six years in, we've been back and forth to Nicaragua multiple times, we've hired a great builder to help us, and the first house is finally complete.

Every goal Jo and I have accomplished in the last few years was on our vision board, and we've used it every day to get back on track. In just a few short years of intentional focus and hard work, we now own seven properties in two countries, and Jo has a great business that allows her to work from anywhere in the world.

Do we wish we were further ahead than we are? Yes. But the hard work I've put in makes it that much more fulfilling.

Life is a struggle only if we let it be. Turning negative events into something educational can give us the motivation and resiliency to keep going. We all learn from our mistakes or from the mistakes of others, and how we choose to react to our wrong decisions, bad choices, or unforeseen circumstances is what really matters. I can't tell you the exact moment I started thinking this way, and there are many times I lost focus. But finding Jo, creating a vision board, and having the will and determination to accomplish my goals have taught me a lot about myself and allowed me to achieve my dream.

In December 2021, we returned to a finished house on Big Corn Island, where we enjoyed a three-month getaway from the snow. This was very different from all our past trips, when I was constantly running a construction project. Finally, all our blood, sweat, tears, and stress have something to show for it. It's an amazing feeling when your vision starts to come true.

We've also been able to fundraise, hire a builder, and start building a house for a local family that didn't have a home of their own. Now that everything feels like it is coming together, I've got even more motivation to start planning additional future rental suites, a bar/restaurant, pool, and bicycle/scooter rental shop. Having our first two suites built means we can finally start generating some rental income and start designing our forever home. We also grow many different fruits, vegetables, and coconuts on the property, and since Jo has turned her health around, being there to take advantage of the healthy island lifestyle is even more important to us.

We decided to name our island property *Drifter's Claim* for two reasons: there used to be a local hangout by that same name in our hometown, where our parents would gather and play live music in their younger years; and the name also connects to the island's mysterious history with various legendary stories of drifting ships and enslaved people landing on Big Corn Island — drifters who claimed their new beginnings. The emancipation from slavery is celebrated every year on Big Corn Island to honor the struggles of enslaved people and to celebrate their freedom since 1841, and as part of the vision we have for the property, we intend to install educational plaques along the rock wall to share and honor this important history with island visitors.

I know having a resort or restaurant wasn't exactly on Jo's radar at first — and there have been a few moments when she wanted to sell. But I'm so close now, I need to keep going. Giving up has never been an option for me. My vision is within my reach now. It's happening. And she's as excited as I am about what we've accomplished and how far we've come.

At a young age, I realized if I wanted anything, I had to do it myself. While some periods of my life felt as though I was drifting, having a purpose gave me the optimism, hope, willpower, and determination to keep going no matter what chaos I faced. I don't let adversity hold me back and every challenge I've conquered has made me stronger and more resilient.

Looking back on what has come from that first vision board and all the ones since, it's crazy to me how something that feels like silly fun could have so much impact. But it does. Maybe the joy and positive energy used in creating a vision board is what makes them work. The excitement of seeing images on a vision board kickstarts the momentum a person needs to really see, feel, and focus on getting real results. Building a dream is never going to be easy, but mine is coming true because of a New Year's Eve party and living my life with a clear vision I see in front of me every day.

About the Author

Mike Boone is from the small town of Wabigoon, Ontario, Canada. He spent his childhood years living with his father in Wabigoon and Dryden, Ontario, and visiting his mum in various parts of Canada until she eventually settled in Lake Louise, Alberta. Mike's first summer job was at the historic Chateau Lake Louise at the age of fifteen, and he gets his love of the hospitality industry and event-planning from his mum and all the years they spent in and around Banff, Lake Louise and Kananaskis. Mike's mum also inspired his love for travel by sharing stories about all the places she has been to around the world.

Despite having a passion for cooking and party-planning, the majority of Mike's career has been spent behind the wheel of logging trucks, long-haul highway rigs, and passenger buses. One of his first bus-driving jobs was with Rocky Mountaineer, where he gave commentary tours while driving tourists through Canada's Rocky Mountains — this experience gave him the confidence for public speaking.

Mike has a love for music and sports, and he has seen many live events including David Bowie, ZZ Top, BB King, a Canadian Football League (CFL) Grey Cup game, and many National Hockey League (NHL) games. He is a lifelong football fan, first as a player on his high school team and since then has been a dedicated Kansas City Chiefs fan — their team logo is tattooed on his arm, and watching a game at Arrowhead Stadium is on his vision board.

Mike and his wife Jo were married in the summer of 2022 and live in Dryden, Ontario with their rescue dog Jemison. Mike also has two beautiful adult daughters from his previous marriage.

Eliminating the financial pressure of living in a high-priced area of the country has given Mike and Jo the opportunity to regrow their Canadian roots while continuing to build additional rental suites at Drifter's Claim, allowing them to focus on living their best possible life.

You can connect with Mike and follow his adventures here:

Website:
www.DriftersClaim.com

Facebook:
https://www.facebook.com/mike.boone.7777 (personal profile)
https://www.facebook.com/Driftersclaimcornisland (Drifter's Claim)

Instagram:
https://www.instagram.com/driftersclaimcornisland/

CHAPTER 13

Are You Dying?

Patti Bevilacqua

Gen walked into my classroom shortly after the end of the school day. From her face, I could tell she had something important on her mind. She dropped like a heavy weight onto the stool beside my desk.

"Are you dying, Ms. Bevilacqua?"

My jaw fell open, and I slumped backwards into my chair. It felt like someone had punched me in the gut. The word "What?" escaped my mouth as I tried to catch my breath. It felt as though all the blood in my head and heart pooled in my feet.

Gen started to speak again, but this time in a whisper. I needed to lean forward to hear what she was saying.

"I play community soccer. A few of my teammates go to the school where you used to teach physical education. We were waiting for practice to start and talking about our favorite teachers. The Pitt Meadows Secondary School girls looked shocked after I said your name. I didn't know you taught PE at PMSS before coming to Garibaldi Secondary School."

I sank deeper into my chair and hoped, with any luck, I'd fall into a deep black hole.

"The students at PMSS think you are dying, and that's why you left without saying goodbye."

Gen stopped talking and waited for me to say something. Instead, I hung my head in defeat; my career as a high school teacher was over. I felt chilled to the bone, but the palms of my hands were sweating.

Gen left my classroom without saying another word. I started to shiver. I felt invisible and numb for the first time in my career. When I had first started teaching, I promised to walk away if I ever lost my passion for it. This is how I felt; I knew my teaching career was over. Being diagnosed with MS really screwed things up. Especially for this die-hard PE teacher. Like other people diagnosed with multiple sclerosis, I've asked myself questions like, *why me* and *what did I do wrong?*

Teaching PE was the only job I ever wanted. I intended to teach high school physical education until I retired. But after that conversation, I knew leaving teaching altogether was my only option. I didn't want people to think I was dying, and I didn't want to keep telling my story to explain why I left Pitt Meadows Secondary and now Garibaldi Secondary too.

So much for the absolute will I invoked to plan, live, and succeed in my professional career. Now what?

Hey, Patti (I often talk to myself). *Do you remember teaching in the School of Physical Education at the University of BC? You were on fire! Teaching others to be AMAZING PE teachers like yourself was your forte.*

Right!

I felt a surge of excitement. Just thinking about teaching stimulated every nerve in my body. I didn't care if the professional career I willed was no longer possible as I knew it. I would find a different way to teach. Suddenly, my heart started beating double time, and the sweat on my palms was from excitement, not stress. I felt the urge to sing and dance. The will that got me to this point was replaced by vision.

In 2001, I started graduate studies at the University of Toronto in Ontario, Canada. I deliberately put myself on the fast track. Usually, people pursuing a Ph.D. take five or six years to graduate, but not me. I was on a mission: to get a faculty position in a college Teacher Education program as quickly as possible. Professors need to pursue robust research agendas and get published in peer-reviewed journals. Securing grants for their research was the priority; teaching was a distant second, which is why most professors are weak teachers. I am not interested in research or getting published. I knew a teacher education program was the ideal place for me.

In 2005 I graduated with a Ph.D. in Teacher Development. My thesis explored the impact of chronic illness on teacher identity and teacher effectiveness. I needed to make sense of what had happened to me, and I found the in-depth process of researching and writing to be very therapeutic, not realizing how much more I was about to learn firsthand in the years to come.

That same year, I got a one-year contract to teach at a private college in upper-state New York. Methods courses and supervising students who were on practicum were my responsibilities. Teaching is at the core of my being and my vision was becoming a reality. And guess what I did at the end of every day? I sang and danced en route to my car.

When I applied for the continuing position the following year, the students and faculty members believed I'd be the logical choice for the job. And so did I. But the department needed a professor to teach statistics. I am competent in physical education pedagogy (teaching methods), but teaching statistics was out of my area of expertise. I didn't get the job. It was déjà vu all over again.

I wasn't going to let this disappointment get to me, and upon my return to Canada I set a new intention: to apply for two positions every month. I figured flying and staying in four-star hotels on someone else's coin would be fun and exciting. I could picture myself sitting in first class. Over the next four months, I applied for eight jobs in teacher education across Canada and the United States. I was interviewed five times by telephone and shortlisted by four schools. I went to three campuses for face-to-face interviews.

Despite my efforts, I didn't get any offers, a harsh reality for a high achiever. I was not accustomed to failure. I cried every time I heard the word "sorry." I couldn't understand why I didn't get the job; after all, I was always the perfect candidate.

Over the next two years, I visited seven more campuses, but the outcome was always the same: I didn't get the job. I hadn't considered the toll this would have on my mental competency. Eventually I got very depressed and filled with self-doubt. I stopped applying for jobs and grudgingly accepted my life with MS despite not knowing what the future looked like for me.

I wandered through life for the next fifteen years. Multiple sclerosis is notorious for its unpredictability, and it is challenging to manage the invisible and visible symptoms. I battled deep depression, dissatisfaction, and disappointment, and I woke up every morning dreading the day. I stopped leaving the house because I didn't want to explain why I was back home again in Maple Ridge, British Columbia. The conversation in my brain was on permanent repeat:

"Hey, Patti. How come you're back? The last time we spoke, you were on your way to teach at some college. What happened?"

I felt like a person who'd farted in public — embarrassed and uncomfortable — and eventually the discomfort became unbearable. I decided it was time to start living and ditch the "poor me" attitude that plagued me every day. I realized that the only one who could change how I experienced each day was me.

I started my journey toward living each day with MS as my best self, no matter how I felt. I read books on self-improvement, mindfulness, and gratitude. I signed up for a beginner's yoga class and an online course titled, *The Power of Positive Thinking*. This course taught me about mantras, setting intentions, affirmations, and mindset. I created a morning and evening routine to begin and end my day in the best frame of mind.

And guess what? It did!

I joined two Facebook groups for women with multiple sclerosis. However, most posts were full of negative energy and the "poor me, why me?" mindset I wanted to avoid. Then, in May 2020, while exploring Facebook, I saw an ad for a free 14-day workshop. The masterclass focused on creating a community to serve a specific niche. The word *community* piqued my interest. The ad got me thinking about the niche I'd like to serve. Serving teachers was not a niche I wanted to focus on because I still grieved the loss of the profession I had always dreamed I would have forever. Not being able to teach left a big hole in my heart.

Once again, I heard the little voice inside ask, *Who else do you want to help? You say you want to make a difference in other people's lives, so who are these people?*

I replied, "Women with MS."

I started to sing and dance again. The jitters I felt in my stomach meant something exciting was about to happen. I immediately signed up for the challenge. Over the fourteen days I named the community, got clear on my message and clear on how to attract the perfect member. I also learned how to create valuable content and engaging posts. It felt great to stretch and use my brain. I had a smile on my face every time I put pen to paper. I intentionally used colored ink so I could put similar ideas together. I also bought a package of index cards. I felt like I was back in school. Singing and dancing became daily events.

I created *MS stands for Mindset Shift*, and the tagline: *Your life is not over; it's only different.* Women around the world and with varying degrees of disability requested to join my group. I created a space online where women with MS can feel safe and understood. I also provided the women in my community with valuable information. I was not formally teaching, but finding a new purpose felt like being reborn — without the soggy diapers.

In eight months, over six hundred members signed up. Whoop whoop! Sixty-eight members are former students from the school where I taught physical education. I never thought I would find purpose and meaning in my life again. Creating this community proved me wrong. But this was only the beginning. I had heard about the power of setting intentions many years earlier, but the foggy disconnect I felt between my heart and head prevented me from giving intentions a try. As it turned out, that online community I created was only a teaser, and the more open I was to possibilities, the more opportunities fell on my plate.

I was living a new life full of substance and significance. I wanted my name to be synonymous with "MS Ambassador." The lessons I learned on my journey were profound. I realized the universe had bigger plans for me all along.

Being openminded and intentionally seeking opportunities with which I align allows me to live each day as my best self while moving closer to my goals. As of 2022, I have authored a chapter in the international best-selling book collaboration, *Absolute Will* as well as this book, *Absolute Vision*; I've interviewed with the MS Society of Canada and several podcasts, including Two Boomer Women, The Hero Within, and the Doug Coleman Show; I was a keynote speaker at a major fundraiser for the MS Bike Tour; I'm a member of 100 Most Powerful Women, One Woman, Sisters Inspire Sisters, and the International Society of Female Professionals, and I am currently preparing to land and deliver a TEDx talk.

Initially, my goal was to teach physical education until I retired, and I didn't need a vision. I didn't understand the difference between the two. I do now: goals are finite; visions are infinite. I know the experiences that got me to this place, but I am not finished. As my vision grows, so do I.

Identifying that my life is not over, it's only different, is the foundation for everything I do now and in the future. By accepting that our limitations stem from a lack of vision and not our abilities, we find the power to overcome obstacles. My story influences my approach to life and impacts my day-to-day physical function, processes, and understanding of self. Though I am passionate about helping women with multiple sclerosis, I believe my message of creating a vision applies to anyone facing a chronic challenge. I want to inspire them to feel a strength they may not have had before and intentionally create the life they desire and deserve. What started with my Ph.D. thesis has come full circle to what I am doing now, and I hope my research and my story will help others weather their storms and find deeper meaning in their journey.

About the Author

Patti Bevilacqua, Ph.D. lives in British Columbia, Canada, with her husband Paul and their two Labrador retrievers, Trooper and Bella. Her entire family is ball crazy. The dogs prefer tennis balls thrown into the water, but Patti and Paul like rugby balls. In 2011 they traveled to New Zealand for the Rugby World Cup, and they have plans to watch the Rugby World Cup in South Africa in 2023.

Patti is a lifelong learner and has a Ph.D. from the University of Toronto in Ontario, Canada. Her thesis research explored the impact of chronic illness on teacher identity, both of which Patti knows well.

Patti likes to walk the local BC trails with Paul, Trooper and Bella. They usually see deer, bears, eagles, snakes, and, if they are lucky, Bigfoot. She is great at telling jokes and believes good things happen to good people. While Patti doesn't let anything stop her from activities she enjoys, if you ask her if there is something she doesn't like, she'll tell you she would rather have a root canal than rake leaves.

Patti is the founder and CIO (Chief Inspiration Officer) of FEARLESS with MS. Her platform is a resource for women with multiple sclerosis who want to live vibrant lives. She shares her experiences and in-depth knowledge to empower women to live with MS as their best selves.

To learn more about Patti, check out her website at https://www.fearlesswithms.com. You can also use the contact form on the website to book her as a speaker for your next event.

Other ways to connect with Patti are through:

Instagram:
https://www.instagram.com/fearlesswithms/

Facebook Group (Fearless with MS):
https://www.facebook.com/fearlesswithms

Email: patti@fearlesswithms.com

CHAPTER 14

The Balance

Tanya Newbould

"I think I want a baby," James said as he poured his morning cup of coffee. At forty, it had already been several years since we decided no kids.

"What? Now you want one?"

"Yes," he smiled. Deep inside my soul, I did too.

Two years into trying, we vacationed in Thailand. Let's just say, "One Night in Bangkok" is not just an 80s song. I found out I was pregnant with a girl. At the time, I didn't know getting pregnant naturally at forty-two was in the 10% category of possibility. Our minds are very powerful and can change our course based on positive or negative information, so I think it's a good thing I didn't know.

The pregnancy went by with ease until I was four and half months along and found myself on my hands and knees, sobbing, with snot pouring out of my nose onto the grey slate kitchen floor.

Well, this can't be normal.

I'm a firm believer if you don't know the "why" of what's happening, it's best to go to someone who can help. I immediately enlisted a therapist to help me take care of my mental health. When the therapist learned I'm adopted, she said, "I suspect your mom was around four and a half months pregnant with you when she realized she had to give you up." My entire body reacted as if I had been punched in the stomach and I found myself in tears again. *Could this be true?* Having had that reaction alone showed me I had some work to do.

As the due date approached, I chose a C-section to play it safe. I was finally getting my bundle of joy and wanted to ensure a healthy delivery. On a crisp September morning we arrived at Cedars-Sinai Hospital in Los Angeles, California, for an 8:00 a.m. delivery. After being hooked up to monitors in preparation for surgery, I listened to all the blips and beeps coming from the machines when my doctor came in to talk about the next steps. Suddenly, beautiful sparkles of light were flying above and around the room.

"What is that?" I pointed to the ceiling.

"What?" she asked.

"The sparkles of light."

She smiled at me. "I don't see it." *Wow*, I thought, *is this my baby's soul getting ready to arrive?* I couldn't help but wonder at the significance of this moment. I was wheeled on a gurney into a very cold surgical delivery room surrounded by a team of doctors, nurses, and anesthesiologists.

Fearing the pain of the epidural shot, I cringed. Surprisingly, it hurt less than some Botox shots I've had. *Rock and roll!*

Soon, the lower half of my body was numb, and the surgery began. Within minutes my daughter was pulled from my belly, and I held my breath until I heard a cry like a small kitty cat's. *All is well.*

I was wheeled off to recovery and James followed the nurses as they took our brand-new little bundle of joy to another area of the hospital to get cleaned up. I yelled to him, "Stay with her!" This was our baby, and I needed to know she wasn't alone. Suddenly my body began violently shaking. I felt as if I'd been dumped into freezing snow with no clothes on. In the recovery room, nurse Jackie put heating blankets on me and set up a heated blower aimed toward me, but nothing worked. I began vomiting uncontrollably. A couple of hours later, a nurse brought baby Ava in, plopped her on me and said, "Time to breastfeed." I was holding Ava with my right hand, holding my stapled incision with my left, and puking into a bucket off to the side.

Six hours later, exhausted, I was wheeled into my sterile room. The mauve curtains buffered the afternoon sun coming in through the window, and there was my baby, sleeping in her white T-shirt, tiny diaper, and pink and blue cap on her head inside a clear acrylic crib. I examined her with awe. *I just had a baby.* Soon friends began to arrive and congratulate us, and it should have been a joyous moment except I didn't feel well. I held her skin to skin, and told myself everything was all right, *but was it?*

We went home four days later, and I was ready to embrace my new journey. I was prepared for the sprint, but not the marathon.

Within three weeks, my joy turned to a downward spiral both physically and mentally. Ava had colic, which turned into a nightly occurrence of her screaming and me rocking her for hours. I withdrew, began crying for no reason, couldn't sleep even when Ava did; I began thinking my friends were against me, talking about me, and even worse, I began repeatedly having visions of throwing my beautiful daughter off our balcony.

I couldn't help but think, *Why would anyone do this to themselves? Why did I have a baby? I'm a horrible mom, my baby is miserable, and I can't do this.*

Three weeks turned into five and a half months, and I couldn't escape the shame and guilt of what I was experiencing. I conjured a plan to fly to Europe and disappear forever, knowing my husband and daughter would be better off without me. Fortunately, when that crisp, sunny Sunday came, I just sat in my car crying, knowing deep down that leaving was not the answer. *But what do I do?* Each time I called my pediatrician, gynecologist, or therapist, I was told to go on anti-depressants or go for a walk. I righteously didn't believe in taking Western medication, and I didn't have the courage to even leave the house for fear of feeling out of control outside of my environment.

Months went by, and life as I knew it was slipping into the abyss. My marriage was teetering, and although I loved my baby and never harmed her, I didn't love myself. I felt isolated and alone. I stared blankly into the bathroom mirror. *Who had I become? If only I could disappear, no longer exist.* A friend had given me Brooke Shield's book, *Down Came the Rain,* but I had defiantly thrown it in my dresser drawer.

One day out of frustration, depression, and desperation, I picked up the memoir and finally started reading it. I devoured the pages, recognizing for the first time what was going on with me. I had postpartum depression (PPD). Not only that, but as I came to learn through a certification course many years later, I had seven out of nine perinatal mood disorders: antenatal depression, baby blues, unipolar depression, perinatal anxiety, panic disorder, post-traumatic stress disorder, and intrusive thoughts.

I searched high and low for information on PPD and couldn't find much of anything. My naturopath prescribed 5-Hydroxytryptophan (5-HTP) and rosehip oil, and two weeks later, standing at my kitchen window overlooking the San Fernando Valley with a clear 180-degree view, I had the thought, *I think I'm okay.* From that moment I began to shift and truly see the joy of having this precious baby angel. My love exploded and I cherished every minute with her, my marriage improved, and I eventually began working again as an actor as well as in my beauty sales job.

I felt whole once more, but I couldn't help thinking there needed to be more information on this mental health issue.

Months later, I was interviewed for a documentary about actors, directed by Jamielyn Lippman. This confident woman before me also had a four-month-old baby. As she was packing up the camera, a light bulb went on in my head. "Jamielyn, I have an idea for a documentary about postpartum depression, and I want you to direct it. I suffered horribly from it and couldn't find information about it. Women need this."

She looked at me with compassion. "I didn't have it, so I don't know if I'm the right person for you." She must have registered my look of disappointment. "Look, I'll post a blurb on one of my mommy websites and let's see if I get a response."

I smiled with relief and gratitude. "Thank you."

The next evening, Jamielyn called me. I could hear the excitement in her voice. "Hey, I think you're onto something. I did a post asking if anyone had suffered postpartum depression and would give a testimony. There were over 100 responses." Tears escaped my eyes, and I got a lump in my throat.

I'm not crazy.

We, along with co-producer Lindsay Gerszt, who was the throughline or central thread of our film, began a seven-year journey to co-create the feature-length documentary called *When the Bough Breaks — a Documentary about Postpartum Depression*. It included doctors' findings, healing modalities, and many women's testimonies, including mine. And guess who narrated and executive-produced our film? Brooke Shields! Her book changed my life, and the goal was to have her be a part of our project. We are eternally grateful for her contribution.

Sadly, at the end of production, one of the mamas who had given her testimony took her own life. She was a very close friend of mine who loved her two kids, her husband, and the Lord Jesus, yet the emotional pain she suffered became too great. Two weeks later, the news came that another woman from our film had taken her new husband's gun and shot herself. It was beyond devastating, and a stark reminder of the importance of shedding light on this relevant subject, truly recognizing the need for compassionate care, screening, and conversation around perinatal mood and anxiety disorders (PMADs).

We premiered our documentary at Dances with Films in Los Angeles. Sitting in the packed audience with family and friends, and seeing the memoriam added for the two mothers who lost their battle, I silently sobbed from the sorrow of my experience and the gratitude for this having become a tangible film to help millions of people. We premiered on Netflix, and our film is now available in 200 countries and six languages, saving lives and families worldwide.

As the years passed and I continued to speak about my journey, the pain eventually dissipated, and I felt more like the wise woman on the hill. I recognized the pain and sorrow in others because I had experienced it in myself. Unlike being an actor, which for me was more myopic and ego-based, with this I had no ego. My only goal is to inform and assist those who need the message. I recognize the importance of what I have been called to do, and sometimes your mess is your message. This is not something I would have necessarily chosen, nor would I wish my experience on my worst enemy, yet I have so much gratitude now for my journey and for having come out of the smoke and into the sunshine.

My experience with postpartum depression, and the subsequent experience making the film, created my vision to change the world. I have been a jewelry designer for twenty years, and I designed a special piece of jewelry called "SOZO Heart," representing perinatal mood disorders. SOZO is a Greek word I heard in a sermon at my church two years earlier and knew I would choose, but didn't know why. SOZO means to *save, rescue, or protect* and it denotes the act of *delivering, making whole, and preserving one safe from danger, loss, or destruction.*

My goal, much like the breast cancer awareness ribbon, is to have over one million women worldwide wear this piece of jewelry with pride from suffering to surviving PMADs, as part of a global tribe and community. This mission has also led me to collaborating on a medicinal candle and diffuser to help target depression, anxiety, grounding, and sleep. Ten percent of the proceeds will go to organizations raising awareness of perinatal mood and anxiety disorders, changing the landscape of the future for women. I've also written my memoir of this grueling journey to let women know, "You are not crazy, you are not alone, and with help, you will be okay."

We are all magnificent souls who have come here to have a human experience. To believe you will never go through suffering, that you shouldn't have pain, or that you are a victim means you are not the creator of your life because you cannot be both at the same time. I believe we come here to learn and grow. Without pain there is no joy, and without darkness there is no light. We are a balance of both sides. The more we can embrace the dark side of ourselves, the more we can then shine. We are the sun, not the clouds that cover the sun from time to time.

With these insights, I began coaching people in 2020 during the lockdowns of the COVID-19 pandemic. The sense of isolation during that time was much akin to the experience of perinatal mood disorders and the old feelings of what I had traversed began to surface quickly. This time, I went on Prozac to balance my emotions as I chose to not show up "that way" for my daughter (again), and balance returned quickly. If you are struggling, take the medication. It's not forever, and I wish I had taken it in the beginning too. As I began to feel better, I chose to commune with others through coaching and create mommy/daughter time daily to navigate this new normal. My daughter truly is the greatest blessing the Lord has ever given me, and I thank God for her every day. I was blessed to thrive through this experience and truly recognize my vision to create a legacy in this world.

You can do the same thing. Sometimes what we think is the worst thing we experience in our life can be the greatest teacher. When you experience strife and you *choose* to not be the victim, you gain wisdom and compassion. You recognize yourself in others and like a warm, cozy blanket, you offer a safe space to those in pain. I love motherhood and everything that goes with it. I learned that when I experience tough times, others do too. When I cry tears of joy for the blessings I have, others do too. When I allow my truth out without fear of judgement, others do too.

I support others to grow and see their true magnificence so they can transform their world and the world around them. That is my core promise. You are whole, perfect, and blessed simply because you were born, and you are here. The scars of pain are also your badges of honor. Wear them proudly, don't hide them with shame, guilt, or excuses.

The time is now, not tomorrow, next month or next year. You have been given one imperfect life, so embrace it fully. The more you stand in your light, the more others will too. This is how we transform the world together, and I invite you to tap into your strength to give others the courage to do the same so we can *ALL* find our vision.

About the Author

Tanya Newbould lives in California, United States and has been an expert in resilience from an early age. She was adopted in the United Kingdom, grew up with an alcoholic parent, and is a survivor of postpartum depression.

A working actor in Los Angeles at the time, Tanya was thirty years old when she met and married her soulmate. Her first foundation has always been her faith in God, but after having her beautiful daughter and suffering from horrific PPD, Tanya was determined to help others. She partnered with two amazing women to co-produce *When the Bough Breaks — a Documentary about Postpartum Depression*, executive-produced and narrated by Brooke Shields.

The film launched Tanya's transformational speaking career and more recently her work as a motivational, trauma and spiritual life coach. Sharing her knowledge and letting others know they are not alone is her passion. Tanya was featured as one of LA's Dynamic Women in Angeleno Magazine, September 2022, and in 2023 she will be releasing the memoir of her postpartum depression journey.

Throughout her adult years, Tanya has always enjoyed creating and designing jewelry, which led to launching Del Pozzo Jewelry. Her stunning pieces have been featured in such publications as Vogue, Glamour, Variety, Condé Nast, Angeleno Magazine, and many more around the world.

This also led to creating the trademarked SOZO Heart pendant, which represents the suffering and survival of women with perinatal mood disorders and postpartum depression, a mental health issue affecting 1 in 5 women, and 1 in 10 men. Like the breast cancer awareness ribbon, the SOZO Heart is a celebration symbol representing mama, baby, and the teardrop of depression. Tanya is proud to also be helping women through the recent launch of a medicinal candle and diffuser under the SOZO Heart brand.

You can connect with Tanya through her websites here:

https://www.tanyanewbould.com/
https://delpozzojewelry.luxury/
https://www.whentheboughbreaksfilm.com/#!/

And through social media here:

Instagram:
https://www.instagram.com/tanyanewbould/

https://www.instagram.com/delpozzojewelry/
https://www.instagram.com/spirituallyinspiredcoaching/
https://www.instagram.com/whentheboughbreaksdoc/

Facebook:
https://www.facebook.com/whentheboughbreaksdoc/

LinkedIn:
https://www.linkedin.com/company/del-pozzo-designs/

CHAPTER 15

When Your Vision Needs CPR

Beverly Jacobson

*B*reathe. *Just breathe.* I could hear ragged gasps escaping my mouth as hot water rained down my back. With my forehead pressed against the glass wall of the shower, I squeezed my eyes shut against the horrifying images tumbling across the movie screen of my brain. The terror continued rising; my chest felt tight. This wasn't my first panic attack, but I certainly wasn't prepared to deal with one during a normal morning routine.

Somehow, I managed to exit the shower and put on my robe. Leaning over the bathroom counter, I inhaled some essential oils slowly, purposefully. Scripture verses, unbidden yet welcome, gradually replaced the terrifying scenes I had been imagining. Hot tears slipped down my cheeks as I reminded myself I had no reason to worry: tomorrow's bronchoscopy was a routine test. The information we could gather from evaluating Verity's airway would help us know how to help her. True, she would be under anesthesia — but this time we would know not to use fentanyl. For some patients, this is a helpful drug. But for our tiny daughter with a life-limiting condition, it is a dangerous substance that had caused her to stop breathing during a minor surgery two months prior.

I looked at myself in the mirror. The weariness would have been evident even aside from the obvious signs of a just-passed panic attack. My husband and I were living in a state of perpetual exhaustion, barely functioning or communicating beyond the minimal requirements to survive.

But I couldn't linger in a state of self-pity. Now that I had collected myself, I needed to set aside my own fears and shoulder the responsibilities I carried as a Mom of Many. Verity's nurse had arrived to care for her, leaving me the mental space (theoretically) to nurture and homeschool Verity's eight older siblings.

This certainly wasn't how I imagined my life playing out. I had always wanted to be a teacher. My childhood bedroom housed a chalkboard and desk, where I taught my dolls and stuffed animal "students." When I was in kindergarten, I wanted to teach kindergarten. With each passing year, whatever grade I was in was the grade I wanted to teach. I finally decided to pursue a degree in secondary English education. I married my Air Force husband with the grand vision of changing the world by inspiring high school students through love of language and literature.

Suffice it to say, my starry-eyed approach to teaching in a public-school classroom collided with reality, but after having three babies in three years and finally emerging from the fog of sleepless nights, I found myself completely, head-over-heels in love with being a mom. Watching my husband be a daddy made me love him even more too. Our marriage grew stronger as we embraced these new parenting roles. I wondered how I could ever send my children off to school — we were having too much fun together at home — so I began exploring homeschooling options. The more I learned, the more excited I became about this lifestyle choice. It seemed a wonderful fit, especially for a frequently moving military family.

In the middle of our first official year of homeschooling, I experienced what may have been the first major crisis of my life. I miscarried a baby at two months. I felt absolutely shattered; I had no idea this could even happen. It was 2006, before social media really came into being, and women I knew did not discuss these topics. A few friends quietly reached out — they, too, had lost a baby. One woman confided that her loss, over two decades prior, still affected her profoundly. My own grief lasted months, only diminishing slightly when I learned I was expecting again.

Four years later, another miscarriage. By now we had five children and had moved several more times. I felt stronger in my faith, though I still grieved this loss deeply. So when my husband announced he was deploying to Afghanistan just after we learned I was pregnant again, I took a deep breath, pulled out my prayer journal, and resolved we would do whatever it took to keep our family strong and thriving during the next thirteen months. After all, we had weathered several deployments already. Granted, none of those had taken my man directly into a war zone...nor had any of them lasted this long.

Although Baby #4 had arrived during a previous deployment, the arrival of #6 nearly pushed me over the edge. My husband was on the other side of the world when the doctor told me our infant son had lost a pound in his first two weeks of life. I cried from exhaustion and stress, feeling like an utter failure. The following months were a blur of meeting with medical professionals, pumping and feeding around the clock, and somehow single parenting six children under age ten.

That year was the longest of my life. Technology that hadn't existed in the early days of our marriage proved to be a double-edged sword: on one hand, I loved seeing my husband during Skype calls. At the same time, I could see the look on his face when he had to end a conversation abruptly because of another rocket attack. I had nightmares about getting "The Knock" on our front door, waking in terror with tears running onto my pillow only to tell myself it was just a dream. My husband was still alive. And, God willing, he would return to his family — including our baby boy who hadn't had a chance to meet his daddy.

Praise God, we ALL made it through that year. Following that deployment, our family enjoyed the privilege of living in Italy for our next assignment. After a stressful year apart, this was a dream come true for our homeschooling family. Gleefully we visited ancient Greek ruins, the Colosseum, European castles, and more. We spent our final Christmas overseas on a Mediterranean cruise, making some incredible memories together. With mixed feelings we returned home to the USA after three years abroad. By now, we had added two more babies to the mix: *mamma mia!* Eight was enough; I was ready to begin the next phase of life.

So I was not exactly pleased to see two pink lines on the pregnancy test I took at forty-one years of age. God and I had some intense conversations about this over the summer of 2016. Just as I began to accept and even feel excited about this final addition to our family, we received devastating news: our little girl had a genetic condition that meant she likely wouldn't make it to birth.

The world stopped. I remember that morning so clearly: all eight children had gathered at the kitchen table for morning prayer and Bible time. The sun shone through the sliding glass door to the backyard, where September warmth radiated from the lush Midwest vegetation. It would have been a perfect morning if it hadn't been for that phone call.

Somehow, we made it through that day. And the next. And the next. And while the rest of my pregnancy with Verity was a roller coaster of emotions, we learned how to prepare for unknowns. We learned how to homeschool while navigating deep, personal pain. We learned how to do life in a fog. The journey profoundly affected everyone in our family.

I would like to say meeting Verity alive and welcoming her home after eighteen days in the NICU brought a happy ending to our story. But the hard part was only beginning. In the early days of my marriage, we had never envisioned having more than two or three children. And throughout all my pregnancies, I had certainly never dreamed of having a child with significant needs. Of course, I delighted in being Verity's mama, watching her overcome statistics. Yet I constantly felt overwhelmed and frightened, expecting her to pass away at any moment.

Perhaps it isn't surprising, then, that a panic attack hit me in the shower on February 4, 2019, just weeks before Verity's second birthday. The episode could have sent me spiraling. I could have slipped back into the stranglehold of depression. I could have given up my long-held, still evolving dreams.

Could have. But instead I came out of that episode clinging to bigger dreams than I ever could have imagined before our season of trauma. I believed in a breakthrough forged in the fiery furnace of crisis.

My vision simply needed resuscitation.

Four months after that panic attack, I wrote and published my first book.

Two years later, I pitched my idea for a nonprofit organization and received a $10,000 grant to launch it.

Four months after launching, I published another book, this one to support our growing ministry to families who receive a life-limiting diagnosis for their babies.

And now? Now I'm growing my own speaking and coaching business, ministering to other homeschool families. I continue building our nonprofit. And I work with a long-term vision in mind: to build a retreat and conference center that will serve both communities.

So what happened between "then" and "now?"

I'd love to give you a step-by-step program or a plug-and-play template to help you walk through difficulties and emerge victorious, achieving your dreams and turning tragedy into triumph. Friend, I wish it were that easy! Looking back, there was no clear path from "then" until "now."

However, I **can** tell you my journey didn't begin in the middle of the muck. The wins and achievements, the overcoming and thriving — all of it transpired because early in life, I made some important decisions. You might say I had CPR training, learning to *center* myself, *position* myself, and then *respond*. You can take this training anytime and set yourself up for success, no matter what storms come your way.

Center Yourself

Whatever your goals are, your vision likely doesn't involve someone you love dying. You probably haven't written "car accident" or "cancer diagnosis" on your to-do list. We can control numerous aspects of our lives, but life is full of unexpected — often unwelcome — surprises.

Trials force us to critically examine our core beliefs. You must center yourself on a foundation of truth, something strong enough to keep you standing firm when life gets shaky. Consider: what is your foundation? Do you believe God created you? Or do you believe everything you see, feel, and experience is the result of absolute random chance? Do you believe we are eternal beings, or does everything end with death? Your answers to these and other foundational questions will shape your thoughts, values, goals, and ideas about success and failure.

These words may seem strange in a world encouraging people to create their own truth. But I don't believe truth is relative. When crisis shakes me to my core, I can press on through the fire only because I have a firm foundation of truth. If I hadn't centered my life on Jesus Christ, I would have made drastically different decisions about marriage and family. I wouldn't have chosen to homeschool. I wouldn't have established a nonprofit. My faith — my foundation — drives everything I do in life, including how I set goals and work to achieve them.

How do you center yourself? Ultimately, YOU have to establish your own foundation.

In what/whom do you trust?
What determines your value?
How do you discover your purpose?
How do you explain suffering?
Is there anything beyond this life?

If you've never considered these admittedly uncomfortable questions, now is the time. Write out a statement of faith that encompasses your worldview — this will shape your personal mission and vision statements. Be sure to discuss this with your loved ones to determine whether you are on the same page regarding your core values and beliefs.

Position Yourself

As a military spouse, I learned to be proactive during transitions. By the time we had boots on the ground, we knew where we wanted to live, what church to visit first, and how to get connected with the local homeschool co-op.

As a mom of many, I learned to establish a workable routine for different seasons of life. Everyone — from teens to toddlers — learned what to do and when to do it. This provided safety for littles, security for older kids, and sanity for Mom.

As you create a vision for your life, setting smaller goals to help you achieve those dreams, how do you position yourself? (This is different from preparing yourself. You can prepare all day long and then never move.) When you position yourself, you take charge of what you can control — rather than waiting for something to happen. You establish the mindset you know you need to move forward — rather than letting your thoughts feed the doubts and fears holding you back.

You don't know what your next crisis will be or when it will blindside you. But if you first *center* yourself on a strong foundation, then *position* yourself to take action, you will create momentum. You'll find it easier to pivot and navigate the unexpected struggles ahead.

Respond

When first responders arrive on scene of an accident, they immediately implement their training. They don't panic or shout. They pull out their tools, work together, and calmly and efficiently attend to critical needs.

When crisis hits, most of us react instinctively. But if we've first centered ourselves on a solid foundation and then positioned ourselves to be ready for anything, we have a mindset that allows us to *respond* rather than react. If we allow emotions to drive us, our reactions might actually make things worse. We could ruin relationships or jeopardize opportunities. Everything we've built could come crashing down in a moment of fear and weakness. It's bad enough when extenuating circumstances harm our family or business, but it's even worse to cause our own downfall because of inappropriate responses.

If I hadn't had a firm foundation from the outset, I could not have positioned myself for future growth and development. My response to trials likely would have been to wallow in despair and self-pity. But instead of letting my dreams die, I resuscitated my vision. Perhaps more importantly, the vision grew bigger — precisely *because of* life's difficulties! Once I was content to teach in a classroom. Now, my vision goes far beyond that: not only do I get to homeschool my own children, but I also teach other moms how to move from heartache to hope.

Does your vision need a little CPR? Invest the time and energy up front — center yourself on a firm foundation, creating a vision that weathers the storms of life. Then position yourself for continual growth and forward movement. Your hard work will pay off when you can respond admirably to adversity.

Center.
Position.
Respond.

You can do this. Your dream is waiting for you.

About the Author

Beverly Jacobson is living out her dreams as an author, speaker, and entrepreneur from her beautiful Colorado home in the woods, where she happily pays someone to clean her bathrooms. She and her Air Force husband have been married twenty-five years and are enjoying growing old (not up!) together. They have been homeschooling since 2005, successfully launching three marvelous human beings who are a force for good in this crazy world.

Though her children have begun leaving the nest, Beverly continues homeschooling the ones who still follow her around asking, "What's for dinner" and "Have you seen my shoes?" She founded Beverly Jacobson Enterprises, a business-ministry that equips Christian moms to speak and live Biblical truth so that they can joyfully and confidently persevere for the long-haul of homeschooling. Her vision is to equip Christian homeschool moms with the most effective, mission-focused tools on the market so they can create a successful, sustainable homeschool, no matter what storms come their way.

As a contributor to the international best-seller *Absolute Will*, the first book in the *Absolute* series, Beverly wrote about the storm that hit the Jacobson family when they learned Verity, their ninth and youngest child, had Edwards syndrome and was not expected to reach her first birthday. After Verity proved statistics don't always tell the full story, Beverly launched a non-profit organization, Verity's Village, which serves other families who receive a life-limiting diagnosis for their babies.

Beverly has authored several books supporting families in these situations, including *Our Baby Will Be Different*, *UN-Planning Our Parenthood*, and the well-received guidebook *From Diagnosis to Delivery: What to Expect When the Unexpected Happens During Your Pregnancy* (all available on Amazon).

You can connect with Beverly here:

Websites:
https://beverlyjacobson.com/
https://www.beverlyjacobsonspeaks.com/ (Event Planners)

Email: Beverly@BeverlyJacobson.com

Instagram:
https://www.instagram.com/beverly_irene_jacobson/

To learn more about the ministry of Verity's Village:

https://veritysvillage.com/

https://beverlyjacobson.com/page/pro-life-speaker (Event Planners)

CHAPTER 16

Cue the Butterflies

Kathy A. Davis

A single tear slid slowly down my cheek. *I saw this,* I said to myself. *It's happening.*

As I paused to soak it all in, I looked around at the tall trees gently swaying in the breeze; the crunchy leaves fluttering to the ground were a sign of autumn. It felt as though the world had stopped, and I was the only one around, sitting under the trees, experiencing the moment I had seen in my mind for so long. I could feel the flutter of butterflies in my abdomen, almost as if they were being released with each exhalation.

The tear symbolized joy, accomplishment, a deep connection with my goals and dreams, and everything I had imagined this risky life decision to be. As I got up from the picnic table to walk inside and tell my husband that *it was happening,* I thought back to how we got here, to this amazing moment.

It had all started eight months before, when we came to the decision we wanted to downsize, sell our house, all our belongings, and move into a fifth-wheel RV with an audacious goal to visit all the contiguous United States and the US national parks. This decision didn't come without much research, planning, or deliberation. Throughout the spring and into early summer, we discussed at length what actions we would need to take to make this dream happen. We immersed ourselves in videos and blogs and spoke with people already doing exactly what we wanted to do. To say we were *obsessed* with it would be an understatement, and that obsession would be crucial in making our vision a reality.

In July 2018, we sat across the kitchen table from our real estate agent, going over the steps necessary to put our 2500 square-foot townhome on the market. The townhome we'd purchased together. The townhome that we loved. The townhome where we had made so many memories in those last five years. The townhome in a city that felt like home to us, and despite not having a house there anymore, it still feels like home when we pass through.

As we put together our list of next steps, discussed numbers, and finalized the plans for listing our house, I felt as though butterflies had taken up residence in my middle. The flutters were unlike anything I had ever experienced. Our dream was moving into reality.

The next morning was humid and sunny; the dew was still glistening on the grass. As I walked into my office, a picture came into my mind: I saw myself sitting at a picnic table under a canopy of trees, just a few feet from the entrance to what appeared to be the RV we had decided we were going to purchase. My laptop computer was open on the table in front of me, and I was typing away, creating content to help my future clients adopt a plant-based lifestyle. A notebook with the details for my plant-based program lay open next to me, with a pen on top. My water bottle was within reach, and the sun shone through the trees.

I stopped walking and looked around to see if others could see the picture too (there was no one else outside). I looked up at the sky and thought, *That. That is what I want. That is where I will work on MY business and the work I am passionate about when we live in our RV. I will keep this mental picture, this vision, in the front of my mind, and one day I will wake up and it will be a reality.*

So every morning that summer, as I walked into my office, I visualized that image in my mind. Each time I saw it, I added more details, like what I would be wearing (a black T-shirt, jeans, and flip-flops), what I would be writing (inspirational plant-based content for my own business to help my clients), and what the temperature would be (around 78 degrees Fahrenheit). I continued to make that picture more vivid in my mind as we worked towards making our dream a reality.

After a month of working tirelessly to clean out the house and move our belongings into the garage to prepare them for a sale, the house was officially on the market. I remember receiving a text from our real estate agent that the listing was live. Again, those flutters of butterflies appeared in my abdomen; it was almost as if they were there to remind me to stay in check with my emotions, to remain grounded, to continue visualizing what I wanted, and not let fear roll in and push me off track. So I paused at that moment, cued my image of me sitting at a picnic table working for myself, and let that vision reconnect me to my goals.

Each night for the next month, I spent time and energy pricing our items to sell. It was bittersweet as I picked up things we had bought together to make our townhouse homier, games we had played, or kitchen gadgets we had used when we cooked together. Despite only living there for five years, we had made many memories, and going through our belongings was stirring them up. If I said every day was easy, I would be lying. There were hard days, and days of fear, but that vision of me sitting at the picnic table, working for myself, kept me moving forward with the actions that needed to be completed.

Mid-September arrived, and it was the morning of "day one" of our garage sale. We were arranging tables in the yard and the garage and beginning to move items onto the lawn when my phone rang; it was our real estate agent. After a quick exchange of hellos, I put the phone on speaker, and the words we had been waiting to hear echoed through our practically empty open loft office: "We have an offer. They want to move fast and close in thirty days." Cue the butterflies — both exhilaration and fear. I didn't know whether to cheer or cry.

She went over the details, gave us her thoughts, and suggested we make a quick decision (the offer was slightly below our asking price, so we had some things to discuss). We agreed to let her know as soon as possible and said our goodbyes. I pressed the red "end call" button on the phone.

There we were, sitting in a desk chair and a camp chair in our virtually empty house, with an offer for someone to purchase our home so we could move into the RV we had purchased just a few weeks before and begin a new adventure of fulltime travel. As I turned to look at John, the butterflies were out of control; not only were they in my abdomen, they were also in my chest. They weren't the only thing in my chest, though; there was a lump; it felt so heavy, just sitting there, almost like an anchor that was holding me down, preventing me from moving forward.

It was fear.

As we discussed the details and how the offer fit into our plans and whether we could make that work, the heaviness eased a bit but didn't go away. The fear was real! I kept looking for the vision in my mind of me sitting at the picnic table, but it was blurred and foggy, like something was "in the way." I paused and mentally tried to clear the blur, the fog, to gain some clarity. It was faint, but I could see it; I could see me.

As we sat there at the desk, I took John's hand in mine and said, "It's our time to leap; we can make this work together." And in that moment, we let our dream and vision of RV life and travel take the reins; we let the excitement push the fear aside. We let our faith guide us toward our vision. And we made the leap. We called our agent back, accepted the offer, and got to work selling everything we owned over the next two and a half days.

The next thirty days were a whirlwind of emotions, movement, packing, donating, social media marketplace sales, and more cleaning out. We were moving from a 2500-square-foot townhouse into a 310-square-foot fifth wheel with a cargo-load capacity limit, so we couldn't take everything; we had to be very selective.

On October 11, 2018, we drove our two Honda CRVs to the Ford dealer, said our goodbyes (I loved my car), and picked up the full-size Ford F-350 that would become the power of our home on wheels. Driving in that big truck was something else, so high off the ground, so much power; it's a beast. That truck made me feel like we could power through anything life tossed our way. I had no regrets even when the butterflies showed up as we pulled onto the highway.

On October 13, 2018, we left our townhouse in our big truck and drove to take delivery of our new home: our 35-foot fifth-wheel RV. While we did our walk-through, the service guys installed our hitch into the bed of our truck so we could safely transport our new home. In just a few hours, we would be making our inaugural tow. We spent about four hours walking through the RV, learning how to operate the slides, awnings, and tanks, finding light switches, practicing setup and breakdown, and beginning our operations checklist for moving days. Our guide said on the last hook-up, "Well, I think you are ready. It's time to take her on the road."

The butterflies were back in full force for me. They had been there all morning, but they were hidden by the excitement of learning all about our new RV. The intensity finally became enough to cause me to stop, take a deep breath, and intentionally bring my picnic table image to the front of my mind.

I'll never really know if John had butterflies. He was so good at keeping his cool. We climbed into the truck with our home on wheels safely connected, and we pulled out onto the road — so symbolic: a road to our new lifestyle. We had already mapped our route to the inaugural campground, so we knew exactly which way to go. As we drove through the country roads of Pennsylvania on that overcast fall day, I knew this "practice weekend" to try out our new life was just the beginning of an incredible adventure.

Over the next two weeks, we moved our belongings into the RV and began to find places for everything we brought with us. I transitioned my fulltime job with another company into a part-time position and began to focus on creating my own business, turning VegInspired "the food blog," into VegInspired, "the plant-based education and inspiration company." We had a hiccup with our house closing, but we didn't let it stop us, and we continued with our plans to start our trek to Florida for the winter at the end of October. Those first two weeks in the RV were a combination of learning how to use all the new-to-us features, getting used to two people working and living in a small space, three cats exploring their spots in our new home, and gearing up for our first long haul out of Pennsylvania. I hadn't known what to expect then, but I can say now that RV life brought more life and inspiration back to me than I knew I was missing.

Our two-week trek towards Florida started on October 27, 2018 and took us from western Pennsylvania through stays in West Virginia, Virginia, North Carolina, and Georgia. It was in Coastal Georgia, just over one week after leaving our hometown in PA, when I realized that holding a vision in your mind helps bring it into reality.

There I was, on a warm southern autumn day, sitting at the picnic table in a campground, writing a piece of social media content to help educate, inspire, and empower more people to eat more plants, when that single tear slid down my cheek and I realized *it was happening*. I was doing the work I'd envisioned while living the lifestyle I'd created. The single vision in my mind that I repeatedly saw and focused upon became a reality at that moment. There I was, actually living it.

As I write this, I get chills when I think about the power of a vision. A vision allows you to see your goals in pictures, it helps you stay focused on what you want, and it enables you to push the fears aside and keep taking action toward that mental image. A lot is backing a vision, but at its heart is your deepest desire. Hold that desire in your mind, see it every day, and let the emotions of achieving it flow into your conscious and subconscious mind. Become one with your vision and watch your desires and dreams unfold before you.

In our travels across the US, people have often said to me, "I would love to be doing what you're doing, but I have a job," or "I have kids," and so many other reasons why they can't. But what if you visualized the reasons why you *can* do it? I have personally used the art of visioneering to achieve many of my life's accomplishments — weight loss, business achievements, authoring cookbooks, and more. Throughout my journey to achieve the "picnic table moment," I pressed on, despite the butterflies and fear, by using that mental image to stay focused on moving towards my goals. I have found that when one uses a clear mental picture or vision, paired with taking action toward a goal or idea they have decided to go after, the achievement rate is higher than for others who focus on lack, fear, or doubt.

One of the most important pieces of tapping into that vision is when you look at the thing you want — whether it's a huge "sell your house and move into an RV" dream, or you simply want to eat healthier foods — circumstances, situations and events pull themselves in to your life. I now use visioneering with my clients to help them adopt a plant-based lifestyle so they can achieve their personal and professional goals. We use writing and visualizing to create clear mental pictures or images of what life would look like for them as they achieve their goals, whether their goal is weight loss, increased energy, or confidence to show up for their audience, family, or career. Whatever their desire is, their results are tremendous when the desire is front of mind and held with belief as a clear vision.

As you embark on your journey toward your heart's desires, pause to create a mental image that evokes emotions for you. What will achieving your desires bring you? What result or outcome will signify that you've reached your desires? Take time to write it out, create the story in pictures in your mind, and let that visual story play on repeat as you take the steps necessary to turn your dreams into reality.

About the Author

Kathy A. Davis is a recipe developer, plant-based lifestyle and mindset coach, and the author of the *30-Minute Whole-Food, Plant-Based Cookbook*, *The Super Easy Plant-Based Cookbook*, and *The Budget Friendly Plant-Based Diet Cookbook*.

Kathy has been eating and creating vegan meals for over eight years and sharing them on her website. Over the past three years, she shifted her daily habits to follow a whole-food, plant-based lifestyle, using the power of visioneering. She has regained control of her health and experienced terrific results: more than 45-pound weight loss, renewed energy, a newfound sense of joy, and a more attuned and thriving mind and body!

Kathy's brand, Veginspired, is dedicated to providing women with the resources to make a similar transformation. She is eager to guide others on their journey to achieve their personal and professional goals by leveraging the power of healthy habits. In 2021, Kathy founded the Eat

More Plants Academy, an elite lifestyle and mindset mentorship program, to educate, inspire, and empower others to adopt healthy living habits with high-touch accountability.

Kathy travels the United States in a fifth-wheel camper with her husband, John, and their cat. Together they have a goal to visit all the US national parks. When she is not cooking up recipes in their little RV kitchen, she can be found writing, bicycling, hiking, or reading with her cat cozied up on her lap.

You can connect with Kathy here:

Website:
https://www.veginspired.com/

Instagram:
https://www.instagram.com/veginspired/

CHAPTER 17

The Making of a Masterpiece

Petar Valkanov

I remember the look on my wife's face when she told me. Like the expression of a startled child when punished for no reason, Margarita's eyes were wide open — clear lakes without a bottom.

I lost my breath. Everything we'd been living for, working for, and dreaming of evaporated immediately. As I hugged her close, the lakes poured out the heaviest tears that have ever fallen on my shoulder.

It's such an insidious, family-destroying diagnosis: cervical cancer. My thoughts began flying around inside my head and I couldn't make sense of what was happening. *How could the human brain be the most perfect computer on this earth and not able to offer a solution right now?*

In our embrace, I could feel the irregular rhythm of her heartbeat in that moment. I froze, imagining there would inevitably come a time when that rhythm would not be there.

Some days the emotional pain was like being hit with a wet rag. The sting of reality was only offset by days when we felt numb and totally empty. Our kids were teenagers at the time, and at first we didn't tell them. How could they emotionally handle what might be the outcome? Was I capable of being a single father? We wanted to protect them from the emotional devastation this would undoubtedly cause, but it became an impossible secret to keep.

When we first told them the news, they didn't grasp the gravity of what was happening — but later, as it sank in, there was a noticeable change in them. They began to show their mother that she was the most loved mother in the world through everything they did. Sometimes a misfortune can change a person's perspective and focus. They went from being primarily concerned with themselves and their own daily lives to becoming caring, mature people and making sure their mother still felt life was as "normal" as possible.

Worldwide, nearly half a million women are diagnosed annually with cervical cancer. Statistics show it is the second most common type of cancer in women aged fifteen to forty-four, and according to the Statistical Institute in Bulgaria, an average of forty-three women per day are diagnosed with it. On an annual basis, three hundred and sixty-five women die from this oncological disease, meaning that on average one woman dies from cervical cancer every single day in our country.

How can you stay strong when you are facing a scary diagnosis and terrifying statistics? It's crushingly heavy on the psyche. I was so afraid of losing Margarita but tried to remain positive as we discussed what the best decision would be for the moment, for the situation.

How does anyone really know what the *best* decision is before you can be sure of the outcome?

Ultimately, as the family tried to come to terms with the situation, Margarita chose to undergo surgery. The doctors had said they could not give a one-hundred-percent guarantee that surgery alone would give us the outcome we wanted and had recommended radiation and chemotherapy, but Margarita refused those subsequent treatment options.

We also began following the recommendations of friends and some alternative medicine specialists. We became vegetarians to alkalize our bodies, we took immune stimulators and supplements, we started practicing yoga and reduced our working hours to reduce our stress. Over the next two years Margarita underwent several additional examinations, the results of which were not what we had hoped for, and a peculiar feeling of powerlessness and unhappiness began to settle on the family. On one hand we had accepted the fate, yet I wandered aimlessly, wishing there was a better way.

Then, one night, something strange happened. I fell asleep, exhausted from the whirlwind of thoughts in my head, and in the morning I woke up with optimism. I was suddenly looking for answers to questions such as: *Why is there unhappiness in human life? Why did no one tell us or give us a sign that Margarita would get sick?*

Past pictures of my life before I met my wife, and before our life together, began to appear in my mind. I went back in time to my late teenage years, a time when I felt terrible. I felt ugly and insecure, with no self-esteem. In those years, also, I had been struggling to understand life and the bigger purpose of it all.

Why does one live?

Why does life itself exist?

What is the worst thing that can happen to me?

What makes me happy?

Pondering these macro questions now with my adult wisdom to guide me, my answers started to emerge, and I began to understand why my wife had become a host for cancer. Margarita and I began to have deep discussions to discover reasons that make a person unhappy and reasons that make a person happy. We realized one can choose to be happy or to be unhappy. Happiness in human existence lies in the balance of the trinity between mind, spirit, and body.

Relationships are the most valuable thing we have. People don't give importance to the little things, especially in modern culture, yet there are no trifles in relationships. Everything is significant. Every word, every look, every emotion either strengthens a relationship or has the power to destroy it. No money, no possessions, no words, and no power on God's scale will ever weigh even one millionth of ordinary human happiness, love, and good relations.

Do not run after mirages and do not tear yourself away more and more from your family oasis of love, care, and tenderness. The real currencies in this world are the time of your life and the health of your body. Use them both carefully, for yourself and your loved ones.

Don't leave the upbringing of your children to people for whom family values mean nothing.

And remember, successful people serve family first. We seem to have forgotten about that.

If you understand these life lessons but you don't have success, is it your motivation that is lacking? I am often asked by friends or clients where they can find motivation to stop eating or drinking certain things, or motivation to change bad habits. It seems everyone is looking for motivation these days, doesn't it? Some have spent years looking for it and still can't find it. I will let you in on a secret: it's nowhere. You can't just go find it. You have to create it by deciding to act. If you are stuck not knowing what action to take, it's more likely that you don't really know what you want. No one can make me do something I don't want, which is why it's hard to motivate another person. So if you have been waiting for others to motivate you, this is why that strategy isn't working. We can't make other people do what they don't want. Neither with good nor with bad, nor with quarrels and swearing, nor with highly intellectual arguments and motivational quotes. You have to mature to find it, yet it's not about age; it's about awareness.

I love this life so much I am not ready to settle for anything mediocre, neither in my physical training workouts, nor in work, nor in my personal relationships. I want the life I am living to be stunningly beautiful. I want to prolong my youth and my health and I'm inspiring others to do the same. This life which we have come to know does not give us the right to a draft. We don't get to re-write it all over again when we get to the end. So why settle for something average (a body that doesn't satisfy you, a relationship that doesn't inspire you, a job that bores you)?

We are all here on this earth with a piece of clay that everyone models differently; some will make this clay into a pile of sh!t, and others a masterpiece. I just want to evolve, a bit every day, to become a better version of myself, even if I must compete with genetics and time.

Waiting for someone else to solve your problems or create a better outcome for you by putting the demands on them is naive to me — a childish position — because your life, your body, and your health are your responsibility. Do you want what you want badly enough? There are no secrets, magic, or motivations. Either you are ready to act, or you are not.

Margarita and I both started to understand the mistakes we had made leading up to the destruction of our life. We had forgotten to love ourselves. We hadn't been giving our bodies the deserved rest we needed, and the physical and spiritual food we had been consuming was processed and dead. We didn't care about the right food for our body, for self-love, for proper communication between us and so many mistakes, which resulted in banishing happiness from our life.

Margarita's diagnosis caused a great upheaval in our family. Our consciousness was suppressed at the time by the solid-black picture fate was unexpectedly showing us. There is a natural law that says to change the result we expect, we must change the efforts we put in. After we changed our attitude to life and started to care about our bodies — soul body, emotional, etheric, physical, auric, spiritual, astral body, mental status — that is when things started to change.

At the end of 2018 and into early 2019, my wife got back to living life and our family began to thrive again. We adopted a new life philosophy and added a *Japanese active hydrogen technology* to Margarita's overall cancer regimen. Her medical checkups began to have better and better results until one day her doctor gave her the most amazing news: everything was clean and normal. It was the end of 2021, and she was cancer-free.

My wife is now full of life and energy and committed to our passion of helping people. We have established a movement we call Мисия Здрави и Щастливи (Mission Healthy and Successful), where we teach people around the world the reasons why their personal health, family relations, and professional life are struggling and how they can improve every area of their life if they have the desire.

Our vision is a world where people know how to lead their life outside of hospitals, far away from processed food, drink the best water with the most effective hydrating effect for their body, know what daily exercises to implement to be flexible, joyful, and active well into their senior years.

We believe everything that happens has a reason and is not a coincidence. We have lessons to learn on this earth and we repeat them tragically until we pass the test successfully. What came to be because of a sudden disaster that befell upon us is now a global mission for us and fills every aspect of our lives. Our mission is to teach people how to improve their physical, mental, and financial health, and to reduce the number of repetitions for as many people as possible on our wonderful planet. Our belief is that every single life on it can be lived longer and lived in happiness and fulfilment, and with this as a guide we are developing a program that will help people become self-trainers and nutritionists.

I encourage you to take a pen and paper and answer these questions:

What does it mean to you to live fully and live in happiness?
What is your "why"?
Why do you do the things you do?

No matter what you think about yourself and the state you are currently in, whether you want to cry or want to laugh and enjoy life, the decision is up to you. Which will you choose?

About the Author

Petar Valkanov is an entrepreneur and motivator living in Pomorie, Bulgaria. He has over twenty-eight years' experience in the corporate world of aviation and over eighteen years of entrepreneurial activity. Throughout his life he has undergone many transformations, which gave him invaluable experience and has now motivated him to help others do the same.

Петър Вълканов е предприемач и мотиватор, живеещ в Поморие, България. Той има над 28 години опит, натрупан в корпоративния свят на авиацията и над 18 години предприемаческа дейност. През живота си той е претърпял много трансформации, които са му дали безценен опит и сега го мотивират да помага на другите да направят същото.

By preaching the principles of his system of cleanliness and health, his followers make sense of the world in which they live and achieve a significant improvement in their lives. Мисия Здрави и Щастливи (meaning Mission Healthy and Successful) is not only a mission, but Petar and his wife Margarita's way of life. Together they have established a global movement attracting people from around the world who want to be healthy and successful.

Проповядвайки принципите на неговата система за чистота и здраве, неговите последователи осмислят света, в който живеят, и постигат значително подобрение в живота си. „Мисия Здрави и Щастливи" е не само мисия, но и начин на живот на Петър и съпругата му Маргарита. Заедно те създадоха глобално движение, привличащо хора от цял свят, които искат да бъдат здрави и успешни.

Petar's business system can help those who want to start a successful direct-selling business, and he teaches how to go from zero to one hundred, how to save time and make profits, and how to avoid the pitfalls of "trial and error."

Бизнес системата на Петър може да помогне на тези, които искат да започнат успешен бизнес с директни продажби, и той учи как да преминете от 0 до 100, как да спестите време, да имате печалби и как да избегнете клопките на „пробата и грешката."

You can reach Petar here:

Email: petar.valkanov100@gmail.com

Phone: +00 359 876267161

Facebook:

https://www.facebook.com/misiyazdraviiuspeshni

(Healthy and Prosperous page)

Facebook Groups:

https://www.facebook.com/groups/academyhealthyandsuccessful

https://www.facebook.com/groups/NewWellnessRevolutionMovement

CHAPTER 18

Precious Milestones

Sonia Aldana Morales

Her name was Angela, meaning "messenger of God." It represented her identity, value, incredible worth, and dignity. Our time with baby Angela on earth was short, but precious.

I was sixteen weeks pregnant when I heard the devastating news. The doctors told me the child growing inside me would be "incompatible with life" after delivery because our baby girl would be "open from the eyebrow to the back." The diagnosis of anencephaly changed the dreams we had for her and our entire family. She was expected to die within minutes after her birth, and there was nothing the doctors would be able to do to save her.

I tried to comprehend the information as a river of tears streamed down my face. *How could this be? God, how can you allow this?* Our excitement had turned to anguish. Why would we be blessed with this baby, only to have her taken away so soon?

I wondered if I would be able to love her, and how I would react to the sight of her deformed head. Then I immediately felt deep guilt.

What kind of mother doesn't love her child? Could I have done something to avoid this? Was this God's punishment? I wept, hating every question that came to my mind.

I spent the following week overwhelmed with emotions. One moment I was in disbelief, the next my husband and I were praying for a miracle, and then there was deep sorrow as we faced the reality of the impending loss of our baby daughter. The doctor had explained that most parents in this position terminate their pregnancy because there was no hope for the baby's survival with the condition she had. For the doctor, abortion was an easy and logical choice. But for my husband and I, this was the baby we had prayed for, a little sister for Elizabeth, and Angela was already part of a family who loved her immensely. It was an agonizing decision for my husband Rony and I to have to make, but we chose to respect our daughter's right to life and committed to giving her dignity. We all die, and at least it would be a natural death surrounded by people who loved her.

The emotional roller coaster was too much to bear. I began losing hope and losing my faith. As I was searching for answers and whatever information I could find, I came across the website *Carrying Colin*. My heart started pounding when I saw baby Colin's face and read about his life. Colin's parents' story showed me that we were not alone, others had faced this journey, and that choosing to love our babies with dignity was worth all the heartache. Colin's precious, angelic face helped me to see beauty in the darkest of times.

In trying to come to terms with the enormity of it all, I felt called to be our baby girl's voice, and a voice of all other unborn babies who are diagnosed with anencephaly and other conditions. I envisioned creating an online community for other parents like Rony and me: a safe place where parents could celebrate the lives of their children, no matter how brief their time on earth. These children would be treated with dignity, loved, and celebrated. Rony and I didn't know what the future held, but we were committed to trusting in our faith to guide us through it. If our daughter was to only live until her birth, we would honor her and give her the best life we could. We created a Facebook community to document Angela's journey.

Angela's impending death was a wakeup call, and reminder that life is short. Life is too precious to waste it on worrying about things we cannot change. It forced me to rethink my own life, to find new meaning, and to realize I needed to focus on living life to its fullest. There is no guarantee that our lives will be easy. Saint John Paul II taught that suffering has value, because it can help refine our character and remove our selfish attitudes towards others. The choice was mine to make as I asked myself, *Do I stay stuck in my sorrows, or do I move forward making the best of every day?* I chose hope and love over fear and found joy in the darkness.

I will never forget the day Angela was born. She was so perfect, so precious. The pain and worry disappeared, and a rush of motherly love filled my heart and soul. Angela was alive. It was a divine moment, filling the room with an absolute joy that surpasses understanding. Two short days later, Angela was already being sent home with hospice care. The doctors had told us, "No sophisticated intervention is appropriate for anencephalic babies," so Angela had been sent home to die. The hospice nurses told us that every movement and sound she made were just involuntary, and that she was dying. But Angela had other plans, and to our amazement she was thriving, proving everyone wrong.

Every minute, hour, and day became a new milestone and a reason for celebration. For twenty-two consecutive days we cut a cake at 6:35 p.m., the time she was born, and we gave thanks for her life. Every day we had fifteen to twenty people visiting us in our home, wanting to meet baby Angela, and celebrating that she was still with us. On day 23, a retired doctor came to visit. She was amazed at our baby's fight for survival, and she offered to help. Rony and I knew we had to become powerful advocates for our daughter. Angela was defying the current literature for a child with a complex diagnosis, so with the retired doctor's help we sought out a new medical team who would give Angela a fighting chance at life. Our hope had been revived, and our daily cake-cutting switched to monthly celebrations instead.

Our love grew for Angela, not for what she was able to do for us, but because she was a member of our family, and regardless of disabilities every human being deserves our respect, admiration, and acceptance. Being a parent caretaker is both exhausting and rewarding. Angela needed round-the-clock care. She was able to eat by mouth; I breastfed her a few times, and continued to pump breastmilk for eleven months as she took a bottle. Children with disabilities show love in many ways; we just need to pay close attention. Angela never spoke a word, but she loved being touched and held. She would often smile and giggle when we held her and cared for her. Her eyes would light up when she heard our voices. While she never spoke, "I love you," she expressed her deep love in her silence and witness to love. We were amazed how our daughter touched so many lives without saying a word. She was a constant reminder to live in the moment and enjoy the people in our lives.

Angela came with us everywhere we went. She went on road trips with us to the beach and to the zoo. She went with us to the mountaintops of New Hampshire. I wish you could have seen her face when we fed the geese at a lake in Maine. This little girl was never supposed to see the sky, but she was in awe when the sun's rays touched her face, when the wind blew her curly hair, and when her tiny toes touched the warm sand. Angela would often smile and loved the life she knew. The ordinary things in life became extraordinary because of her.

And what parent doesn't get excited about the first day of school? I cried tears of joy when I saw her going on the school bus to pre-kindergarten where she could have friends and be immersed in an all-inclusive classroom with other children with disabilities. There she was at age three, lifting her little hand to press the red button on the adaptive toy. Milestone after milestone, Angela motivated us to live every day as if it was our last.

Despite our hopes for Angela's survival against the odds, we also knew a life of breathing machines was not what we wanted for her. We prayed for the grace and wisdom to advocate for any medical treatment that would help her live and have the best quality of life, yet we also trusted in God and in Angela to show us when she was ready to go. And she did. As painful as it was, when she became ill and started to show us she was tired, we recognized she was telling us her time was short. We chose palliative care, and we are grateful that she received the most compassionate, loving care at the end of her life. Angela lived for three years and eight months, happy and content with her family.

A few months after her passing, we learned Angela's palliative care doctor was educating medical students about the beauty of embracing life. Angela was a child, not a diagnosis. Angela's time on earth may have been short, but her life had an impact not only on our family, but also on the broader medical community. Her palliative team wrote in Angela's obituary, "Angela taught her family, friends, medical community, and the world lessons on how to live a life full of love and appreciation. She taught through unspoken words, in a way more powerful than any book ever could." Without ever saying a word, she became an ambassador to others around her.

No parent ever wants to lose a child. But losing Angela prompted Rony and me to re-evaluate our lives. As much as it's been the most painful, overwhelming, and never-ending journey we've had to endure, there has been love and joy amidst the pain. Pain is not always undesirable; it can also serve a purpose. We've experienced unconditional agape love: divine love. The love for Angela keeps growing and overflowing and fuels my passion to keep her legacy alive. We grieve because we loved. How blessed we are to have experienced that kind of love — pure, divine, and holy.

Those years I spent caring for Angela, I gained more self-awareness and an increased ability to see the joy of life. Walking this path also helped us develop great strength and endurance as we came to terms with the grief we were experiencing. There is so much we can do to get stronger every day, but parent caretakers sympathize that at some point our strength just isn't enough. This forces us to recognize that alone we can't overcome adversities because at such times we are elevated beyond our limitations. God was my strength, holding me together. If it wasn't for my belief and faith, I don't know where I would be.

I learned how vital family and friends are, and that you will find joy and miracles everywhere if you look closely, even after enduring the most unimaginable grief. It is possible, and it is a process, but you will get there. I started living more intensely, more deeply, as life now has greater meaning and purpose. Every day is a precious milestone, to live the best life we can.

Pain taught me to seek help from others. It forced me to see beyond myself and my personal suffering and led me to find strength to look at the suffering of others. I never expected I would meet so many other moms on the same journey I experienced. I would encourage you all to be brave and to be that unwavering advocate for your child. You will meet teams of medical professionals who see a diagnosis and don't see the dignity of your child. There will be days when the emotions are overwhelming, and you want to give up. No matter what, keep going. Your child deserves everything in life.

Eight years ago, I had a small vision to share Angela's story with other parents: to offer words of encouragement, support, and to be a listening ear. In doing so, I realized that sharing our experience is incredibly powerful; it helps us heal, and we can start to respond more compassionately. It enables us to move from an egocentric focus on our personal hardship towards a broader focus of helping others. Today Angela's story has reached a Facebook community of over 20,000 followers across forty-eight countries, and we share valuable resources with other parents who have received a limiting diagnosis for their child. Our community walks with them on their journey, raising awareness for anencephaly and other disabilities. I am honored to share the gift that Angela's short life was to our family, and to the world. I'm also currently working with a faith-based community center helping women who are facing a crisis pregnancy. Sometimes these moms are in vulnerable situations, facing homelessness, domestic violence or have received a grim prenatal diagnosis for their unborn child.

My vision for my family and my future is completely different than what life was like before Angela. Reflecting on my life before the diagnosis, I was still learning about motherhood. I hadn't grown up in a stable household and I held a lot of resentment. When our first daughter Elizabeth came along, I parented her the same way I had been raised: without showing love and affection. When Angela was born, my dreams shifted and I had to relearn what motherhood is all about: patience, self-sacrifice, and unconditional love. Our family — and my mindset — continued to grow while Angela was with us, and since her passing. While some days are understandably messy with three children and another on the way, my perspective now is that motherhood is a sacred, empowering journey.

I have become a public speaker, serving as an advocate for perinatal palliative care and prenatal diagnosis services through the sharing of Angela's story. I am taking Parent Care Coordinator training to learn about trauma-informed care to provide continuing support and advocacy throughout pregnancy. I can testify that carrying a pregnancy with a life-limiting diagnosis is ultimately better for the mental health of the mother. I carried, nurtured, and gave birth to my daughter Angela not knowing how long she would live, or how she would change the world, but the time we had her with us changed our family forever. We were able to know her, and provide the dignity she deserved until the moment she died in my husband's arms, surrounded by those who loved her. This difficult journey has molded me into the person I am today, and I wouldn't be who I am if it weren't for Angela.

About the Author

Sonia Aldana Morales is an author, bilingual public speaker (Spanish and English) and a community advocate for prenatal diagnosis service and palliative care for babies who are expected to die after birth. She and her family live in Rhode Island, United States. Sonia is thirty-five years old and has been married to her wonderful husband Rony for fourteen years; they have four children and another on the way. Angela, their second child who was the inspiration for this chapter, died five years ago at the age of three years and eight months.

Sonia has served in the community for over ten years and is fiercely determined to help women in need. As a community health worker and local program coordinator for pregnant and breastfeeding mothers, as well as infants and children, Sonia assists families to reach their fullest potential by helping them see their worth and giving them hope through sharing her own story. Sonia coordinates services and collects resources for women facing homelessness, abandonment or experiencing a crisis with their pregnancy; she volunteers at a local pregnancy center as an interpreter, has coordinated baby showers and toy drives, and she has organized multiple fundraisers to support women and children who have life-threatening or life-limiting illnesses. She is also an active member at her church, serving at women and marriage retreats.

In 2019, Sonia and her husband Rony received the Lumen Gentium Catholic Service Award for their service in the category of Respect Life — serving the poor, advocating for justice, defending the gift of life and for helping the community in need.

Sonia loves speaking about the gift of Angela, from the prenatal diagnosis, birth and caring for her child until Angela's natural death. Sonia speaks in conferences, schools, churches, and other organizations.

You can reach out to Sonia at:

Email: sonia.aldanam@gmail.com

Facebook:
https://www.facebook.com/Angelacarrytobirth (pro-life speaker page)

Linktree:
https://linktr.ee/soniaaldana

CHAPTER 19

The Road to Me

Mimi Hricko

"I experience you as fake."

WTF!? Well, I experience you as a judgmental a$$. You know nothing about me, so your superficial opinion is obviously a reflection of past experiences of rejection. Idiot.

My eyes darted back and forth, glaring into each of the instructor's pupils. My jaw tightened as my teeth clenched. My heart raced and my throat stiffened as my body surged with adrenaline. Yet, during this unconventional personal development conference, I compelled myself to keep my desired response unspoken. Regardless of how we were perceived, the group had been instructed ahead of time to only reply with one simple phrase: "I acknowledge your position, and I promise to weigh it carefully before taking any action."

Therefore, I regurgitated the prescribed foolish statement. In doing so, this man's opiniated allegation plunged me into a road-not-taken journey: at forty-four years old, I would set out on an excursion to evaluate my most significant relationship.

Five months before this experiential seminar, I had left my marriage of more than twenty years. While I had been slowly realizing and understanding the hidden abuse I was enduring, guilt and hope kept me attached. I had eventually come to a fork in the road, a point of decision at which I grasped that pain would be unavoidable regardless of the direction I took. I finally accepted there would be no reprieve from the inescapable ache of my current situation. And so I switched my course. I chose the discomfort of grief necessary for healing, so I could be relieved from the anguish of inflicted harm. However, I did not anticipate my genuineness being called into question while on this positive progression of personal growth. Yet, despite the bitter emotions the instructor's words provoked in me, I weighed what he'd said to me carefully. It was heavy.

For two decades, many aspects of my existence *were* fake. Covert mistreatment requires a façade by the abuser and their victims. Without notice, my own identity had faded away as I protected the reputation of the man I married.

My vision for my own life was always there. Yet my spouse had managed and molded it according to his agenda. Early in our marriage, I shared my desire with him to write, speak, and motivate others. His response to my dream was one of many confusing compliments he used to coerce control: "No, you will be successful at whatever you do, and I don't want to be in *that* spotlight."

With that, I submitted both psychologically and spiritually. Yet the infractions against my autonomy continued, craftily weaved so that my sense of self diminished over time. I had become untrue to myself.

But now, as I considered the trainer's perception of me, piercing yet simple questions engulfed my head, my heart, and my soul.

Who am I and how did I get here?
Where did *I* go?
WTF happened to me?
What now?

As I began to answer these questions, the epiphany from the experiential seminar and the "idiot's" brilliant observation propelled me to move forward with determination like never before. The methodical aspect of my personality led me to investigate techniques and tools for happiness. I elected to focus on the dimensions of wellbeing which I thought would be the key to curing the chaos I had come to exist in. I would reclaim everything my ex had taken from me. I would finally practice what I couldn't wait to preach. I was ready to be my authentic self.

I trotted along the unworn path of an alternate reality for my future. I began to feel the fresh, greener grass softly tickling my childlike soles. I was thriving in every aspect of my health.

Indeed, I had the best year of my life! I was on top of the world.

The physical, financial, and social pieces of my picture-perfect wheel of delight were prospering. I was stronger and healthier than ever. Symptoms I had suffered for years due to the chronic stress of abuse ceased. I committed to being fit and found freedom from depression, intense neck pain, and explosive tension headaches. Because I no longer had to manage my ex's spending or addictions, I purchased a vehicle without the fear of monetary sabotage. I felt a cool gust of relief at retiring a nineteen-year-old minivan. I no longer had to drive with no air conditioner in 100-degree weather, as I'd done for years. I built relationships and had fun! Whether it was a week in New York City with one friend or grabbing dinner with a bunch of buddies, who knew I could laugh and responsibly drink without having to stay on high alert to manage someone else's alcohol and behavior?

In addition, the spiritual, emotional, and mental pieces of my wellness wheel also flourished. Freedom from misplaced submission allowed my spirituality to begin healing. I began to serve others again. Even so, I'm sure a trip to Puerto Rico to help rebuild after hurricane damage brought more peace to my internal whirlwind than to those affected by the literal storm. I became intensely involved in that experiential seminar which previously had made me angry enough to find my joy! Being on the other side of the table, helping others, contributed to one of the most emotionally fulfilling years of my life. My intellectual power also ignited. While married, supporting my detractor's career became *our* priority. Therefore, two years into the union, I had abandoned my college studies. I had also walked away from seven years of active-duty Air Force service. But now, after a nineteen-year separation from the military, I would re-enter the Air Force Reserve at forty-five years old, and I looked forward to completing my degree.

The divorce was final one year, one week, and six days after filing, and life as I now knew it was only getting started. Everything was perfect. With my newfound bliss, I embarked on what I anticipated would be a two-year endeavor: one year on Air Force orders and one year of civilian education. My motivation was high. After all, part of overcoming the control of the life-depleting marriage would be to show him he could no longer stop me from fulfilling the vision for my life. I just knew proving to him that he didn't kill me, or my dreams, would facilitate my recovery immensely. Escaping the past didn't mean running away. True escape meant running toward the future. Nothing could go wrong as I lived my best revenge life.

Two and a half weeks into a six-month Air Force technical training, I embraced a Saturday sleep-in. As I was lounging on this rest day, my cell phone rang. It was my son.

I cheerfully answered, "Hey, sunshine!" And while his response was a simple "Mom," the tone sent chills down my spine. There had been an accident. And before the next hour had passed, we knew the outcome: after twenty years of marriage, one year of separation, and less than ten months divorced, my ex-husband died.

A yearning only a mother could know consumed me. Being away on military orders, I could not be physically present to embrace my babies during such a moment as this. My children and I had already been following our own paths of healing, but now confusion, doubts, unresolved closure, new emotions, and additional trauma muddied our recovery. The sadness of today does not undo the sadness of yesterday, but it does provide another fork; it offers another road-not-taken opportunity.

The remainder of that year continued to disprove the "nothing could go wrong" story I had anticipated when I was high on life just a short time ago. My mom learned she had colon cancer, leading to two surgeries and a couple of months of touch-and-go fear. I also required surgery during that time, which added to the demand as her primary caretaker. Furthermore, I lost relationships and an essential support system when I needed them the most. The best year of my life had been followed by one of the worst. But while a revenge life was now irrelevant, my vision was still intense. My eternal optimism and my lifelong dream would not allow me to stall for long.

The following two and a half years would prove to be both triumphant and challenging. I accomplished lifelong goals: completing my Psychology degree, earning my Life Coaching certification, and becoming an international best-selling author. Yet interspersed with these achievements, I had been suffering from exhaustion, joint pain, insomnia, weight gain, and more, culminating in two more surgeries. And now my beautiful, brave mama was also managing metastatic breast cancer.

A two-year endeavor I had anticipated to reach the launch phase of my aspiration turned into three and a half years. Along the way, I experienced severe self-doubt and wondered if I was genuinely qualified to coach others. There were times I questioned if the training instructor's words years ago still rang true. *Was I fake because I now sometimes cried over particular good memories with my abusive ex? Was I fake because I couldn't always override negative thoughts with mantras of positivity? Was I fake because I sometimes questioned my country even as I wore combat boots? Was I fake because on bad days unicorns and rainbows could trigger me? And what the hell does "be your authentic self" even mean?*

Eventually I identified something even more significant than external credentials alone could provide. I realized that while I never intended to live a fake life (in my marriage or otherwise), I also never set out to live a real one.

I found that just as we acquire a language, we also learn what to think, how to feel, and what to do. I discovered the consequences of suppressing our emotions, not recognizing the signals our bodies provide, and not understanding the effects of familial and social influences on who we are. We assume characteristics and often don't notice or question this conditioning. We then live out "fake" identities by default. It's not that we are being inauthentic. We sincerely show up with the level of internal awareness, acknowledgment, and acceptance we have in any circumstance. Alas, what we have learned does not always serve us well. Fortunately, we have absolute jurisdiction to unearth the impacts of these subliminal authorities on our identity.

As we stroll, prance, run, crawl, and sometimes get pushed down the trail of human life, we can glance back to explore the past with hindsight. This enquiry is not to dwell on what happened then, but to be thoughtful with what is happening now, and to create intentional reverberations into our future. Our power and peace coexist when we explore the life we have lived with compassion, grace, and curiosity. Only then can we understand that in every moment, we are who we are because of who we were, and we get to decide who we want to be.

As a result of my passion for learning and all I discovered through my own personal growth, I created a framework that allows us to expand our level of awareness, acknowledgment, and acceptance of each aspect of our individuality. It provides the *how-to* for the cliché: "be your authentic self." I now get to help others gain individualized insight and the ability to cease being bystanders in their own lives. Everyone deserves the opportunity to explore who they were always meant to be through a clear lens. When we uncover what formed our identity, we can begin to live in our *deliberate* truth and not by our *conditioned* defaults. There is absolute freedom when living with an unapologetic agency and our vision becomes clear when we are no longer escaping ourselves.

The road not taken is not the high road, and it's not necessarily the less-taken road. It is simply a different route to the same destination on our expedition through life. It allows us to be aware of, acknowledge, and accept everything within us and everything that surrounds us, even when the passages are muddy and messy.

When the brilliant training instructor cared enough to perceive me as fake, he saw something I had yet to see. He thrust me into weighing my most significant relationship: the one with myself.

My dream was never about living a life of vengeance.
My absolute vision is living a life of victory.

And now, what matters is how I experience me.

I experience myself as curious, detailed, and tenacious.
I experience myself as versatile, relatable, and adaptable.
I feel and think deeply.
I am intuitive and deliberate.
I encourage and inspire.

I seek purpose passionately.

I am strong. And I am weak.

I am independent. And I need the collective.

I am everyone.

I am no one.

I am uniquely me.

I experience myself as a resilient, beautiful, brilliant badass.

I love who I was, I love who I am, and I love who I am becoming.

I experience *all* of me, and I experience myself as real.

About the Author

Mimi Hricko is a professionally certified Life Coach, speaker, and international best-selling author. After years of living in both deliberate and unintentional denial about trauma and repeated patterns, Mimi finally discovered what would allow her to become her truest self. Based on her journey of personal growth through various generalized modalities, she has created a unique tool and a proprietary framework to help others gain individualized insight into their own lives. Her process provides the *how-to* for the cliché "be your authentic self." Mimi has embraced being appropriately unapologetic and is passionate about helping other women achieve the same.

Mimi has a Bachelor of Arts is Social Psychology. Her current certifications include mindfulness-based cognitive training from the Life Coach School, and an Advanced Certification in Feminist Coaching. She has also been certified as a Resiliency Trainer and has studied nervous system regulation. During 2018 to 2020, Mimi was a primary trainer for the experiential seminar Focus Seminars of Kansas City. From 1998 to present, she has mentored and coached hundreds of women on life and business topics through her two businesses. She was also a co-author in the international best-selling collaboration *Absolute Will.*

Mimi is dedicated to walking women through an intense yet amazing process of fully discovering or reclaiming their power and identity. If you look at any part of your life and say "WTF," consider working with Mimi to discover your authentic path to YOU. It is not time to start over. It is time to stop compartmentalizing yourself into past, present, and future beings. It is time to meet, embrace, and adore yourself completely. The awareness that who we *were* impacts who we *are* allows us the power to choose who we *will be.*

Mimi is a native of Philadelphia, Pennsylvania, United States, but landed in the Midwest where Kansas City has been her home for the past twenty+ years. For short periods of time in between, she lived in Texas, Iceland, and Idaho. Mimi is a mom to two astounding humans who are both married to remarkable individuals! She is also an Air Force Active-Duty Veteran and currently proudly serves in the Air Force Reserve.

For up-to-date social media presence, resources, opportunities, and ways to connect and work together, please visit her website at https://www.mimihricko.com.

CHAPTER 20

Soul Seeking Expression

Daniela Panetta

I *sn't there more to life than this?*

Many days, that was one of the questions I found myself asking. For as far back as I can remember, I felt that there was more to life than how I was living, and the longer I went without addressing this within myself, the worse I felt. My vocation as a registered pharmacy technician had been a "good choice" — a career that would always offer job opportunities. But it wasn't giving me the same satisfaction anymore. I had gone into the profession to help people live healthier lives, but as the years went on, I began to see myself as nothing more than a professional drug dealer. Medicine can be used for a great cause, but most medications are just a Band-Aid covering up a problem; they are not the solution.

My job had little to no room for growth, and I still had fifteen years left before I could start collecting my pension. My mental health was deteriorating as I tried to cope with the day-in-day-out struggle of my unfulfilling existence, knowing how much longer I had to stick it out for. I would spend hours wondering why we hold ourselves back from living a life that is truly ours, wanting to understand why fear is so deeply instilled within many of us, while continuing to go to work every day to a job I knew I didn't want. I didn't feel as though I were truly helping people, and I was just going through the motions. I wasn't fulfilled anymore, but I also wasn't ready to make a change.

Society has built a box that we all are expected to fit into, but those walls don't work for everyone. The box of expectation wasn't working for me, and yet I was scared of losing everything I had worked so hard for, scared of failure, and scared of what people would think of me. I often asked myself: *Who am I? why am I here? and what is my purpose?*

I identified as someone with anxiety. Worrying about the future was my specialty. Worrying is like asking for something you do not want but you get it anyway. I felt stuck in the cycle of the fear, a lack mindset of dwelling on the things I didn't have and the rat race to retirement. Talk therapy sessions and the offer of prescription medication were presented to me to combat the fear and worry. I was not interested in that type of approach in a system that doesn't give people the support to discover what the deeper issues are. I wanted so much more than that. I wanted to know why and where these thoughts and feelings were coming from, not just cover them up and ignore them, and eventually I came to the realization I wanted to be able to help other people answer these questions as well.

Every day after my morning work break, I would walk along a glass bridge that led back to my department. I would stop and gaze out the window at the sky. I would think of all the things I was grateful for, and I would ask my late father for guidance and direction. I can remember thinking there was no way I came here to this world to work in the basement of a hospital, dispensing medication for the rest of my life. I asked the creator of the universe for some sort of message, or sign, as to the next steps towards living a life that would make me truly happy. I wanted to know why I was here and how I could be of service to others questioning their own existence, who want to create a better, healthier life for themselves.

My career came with all the so-called bells and whistles. To leave and pursue other work would have been crazy. I knew it, my family, friends, and colleagues knew it, and words like "safety," "security," and "pension," played like a broken record in my head, louder and louder, every time I shared my feelings with others. I was constantly reminded to "play small," which further instilled fear in me, with a side of self-doubt.

Now, don't get me wrong: there were certain aspects of my career that brought me great satisfaction, but there was also something deep down inside screaming for a different life. I wanted a life with more meaning, purpose, and fulfillment; a life that was mine, not a life lived on autopilot. The simple, mundane tasks we perform each day such as washing our face, brushing our teeth, and putting our jacket on, are all just mental programming from years of repetition. You probably do them in the same order every time, right? The right arm goes in before the left — or it might be the other way around — but whichever way it is, the program and the order are embedded in your mind. You just do it; you don't consciously think.

The constant repetition of these tasks allows our brain to go into autopilot mode. Have you ever driven home from the grocery store and pulled into your driveway, only to realize you don't recall the drive? This is because when you got into the car at the store your mind brought up the "mental program" to drive you home. We have many mental programs, most of which are habitual, and most of the time we are not consciously thinking about what we are doing and creating. I didn't want to be so disengaged anymore because it had started to feel as if there was no point to any of it, and yet I knew there just had to be more.

When you choose not to live life on autopilot anymore and you start to create your new life, the new mental programs do not exist yet. You have to create them, and doing that can feel overwhelming and scary. Changing anything takes intention, and change as big as this takes time, patience, and consistency to create a life for yourself that really excites you — one that you genuinely love living.

"Excuse me, what did you say — create a life for yourself?" That still sounds crazy to me sometimes when my old programming pays me a visit. Growing up, most of us, myself included, were told to go to school, get a career, get married, buy a house, have kids, and get a pet — so many expectations, and if you did them out of order, it meant you were veering off the path. Then we are supposed to retire mortgage-free with a big fat pension and live happily ever after. Our success feels like it is gauged on how many of those milestones we hit, with bonus points if we achieve them by a certain age.

Who made these rules anyway? I sure didn't.

I lived nearly forty years by these limiting rules, and they weren't sitting well with me anymore. We've been conditioned to just go through the motions: to wake up in the morning only to dread going to work, to go home to eat, to watch Netflix, to work fifty weeks of the year just to look forward to two weeks of travel, and to live paycheck to paycheck. This isn't living; it's merely existing. I did not come here to "just exist," and I was tired of accepting that bleak reality for myself. There was no way this was the end-all-be-all for my life.

It feels like yesterday that I was terminated from my fulltime, eighteen-year career in healthcare. There's a saying to be careful what you wish for because you will receive it. If I hadn't already been wondering what more was out there for me, for my life, and asking for a sign, I might have been devastated or thought my life was over when my "wish" came true. Instead, I took it as an opportunity, a road to get me from where I was to where I wanted to go.

I knew deep inside this was happening *for* me, not *to* me; it's a concept that can allow us to be more open to taking the next steps when life throws us a curveball. When we look at challenging situations from a perspective of opportunities and lessons, as opposed to having a victim mindset, it changes the thought process from negative to positive and can bring us clarity. This technique can also help us cope with the stress that might come from these types of significant life events.

Though I was still trying to make sense of what had happened, I decided it was time to embark on a new adventure and pursue my vision of living bigger and better, and to help others do the same. This was part of the plan, after all. In the last several years at the hospital, I had decided I wanted to start a side gig as a coach, but I wanted to match my yearly income before I transitioned down to part-time at the hospital or left my career altogether. Losing my job was unexpected and sped up the timeline; I knew it would be a rocky road, but I had faith I was being led in the right direction.

Faith is the ability to believe in something you cannot see. For many years I had lived in fear: fear of failure, fear of loss and most of all, fear of not being accepted. The truth is fear does not exist when you are your true, authentic self. Once I understood I am the creator of my own reality and that I have the ability to live a free and abundant life, things started falling into place for my life and my new career. The right people began coming into my life, my mindset shifted, and I am no longer living in a state of fear and worry. What a life-altering time this has been so far.

I've come to understand that the path the less traveled is a forever journey. It might feel easy and more comfortable to stay the same, but if we avoid pushing ourselves there will be no growth. Without growth, we are more likely to continue playing by the same old rules and following our conditioned patterns. Learning to become the best version of myself hasn't been easy, and at times, when I haven't surrounded myself with the right people cheering me on, who see my vision, it has felt pretty lonely. But I've realized that the key is to live in the present moment, and I've developed a strong belief and faith in the process.

I've been studying books and material to develop my mindset for several years, and this continual learning has been pivotal to my growth, my mental health, and my new career path. I am a forever student but now I am also a coach. I am taking everything I've learned and all the adversity I've overcome and I'm using it to help others move through what seems to be impossible for them, to help them create unstoppable confidence and start living the life of their dreams.

It's possible to achieve greatness. It's possible to create that life you think about every day. If there's a vision within you of a life you want to live, there's a reason you're having the thought in the first place, and it's possible for you to create it. I know it may be hard for you to believe in yourself some days, so I encourage you to borrow my belief until you do. You do not have to figure this out on your own; worrying about the "how" was exactly what held me back for years until I began growing my mindset and accepted the idea that a coach could help me get to where I wanted to go much faster than trying to do it on my own. Though I had thoughts of fear and failure, I also knew I didn't want to be stuck in the same cycle for years to come. I realized I had to invest in myself to create the change I was looking for.

Failure only exists when you do not take action to start reaching for your goals. I'm so grateful I overcame my worries, fears and struggles, and now I've made it my mission to help others break free from a life that was created for them, not by them. I've started living my life on purpose, rather than on autopilot, and since becoming a coach myself, I've felt more fulfilled and purpose-driven than ever before. I'm not giving people a Band-Aid anymore that I *hope* will help them; I know I really *am* making a difference by working with them to discover their own solutions. And there is so much more empowerment that comes from this process.

Whatever you're going through right now, it's happening on purpose for you to become the person you were created to be. I believe we all have a burning desire deep down inside ourselves; it's our soul seeking expression, which is always for expansion and a higher good.

Start taking action towards living a life that truly matters to you, and doing something that aligns perfectly with your values and beliefs; follow your passions, give back to others, set goals and strive for a more balanced life; find meaning in the little things so you can appreciate what you have and be present in every moment of your life; ask the right questions, and surround yourself with the right community. Having a coach's guidance helped give me the belief and faith needed to move me along my path in finding my happiness.

I'm constantly growing into who I am and realizing why I'm here. Your dreams are calling you. You either pursue them or you're haunted by them. We are in control of our life through our thoughts, feelings, and actions but we need to let go of the "how." Life has a way of unfolding even better than we could ever have imagined. Be open-minded, stop worrying about what you don't want, and start taking ownership of what you do. It's time to get rid of the baggage, the junk, and the self-sabotaging talk telling you you're not good enough or that you're crazy to want something more out of life. It's time to release your limiting beliefs one by one. There will never be a perfect time, so make the decision that the time is now.

About the Author

Daniela Panetta is a daughter, sister, friend, author, program facilitator and speaker from southern Ontario, Canada. She is fun loving, outgoing, and an animal lover and nature enthusiast.

Daniela is a certified mindset coach, success consultant and a retired registered pharmacy technician. She has committed herself to supporting others in raising their consciousness and reclaiming their power by creating a healthy lifestyle through natural remedies and healing modalities.

Daniela is a published co-author in two books: *Your Wake Up Call,* by Joe Trimboli — a collaboration of life changing stories helping people to wake up to what's possible for them — as well as *Absolute Vision.*

Daniela's mission is to help people worldwide break free from a life that was created for them, not by them. This is achieved by helping them rediscover their passions, gifts and skills to transform their life to create more personal freedom.

Connect with Daniela today to find out more about her 1:1 coaching, courses, programs, books and upcoming events:

Instagram:
https://www.instagram.com/daniela.panetta_

Linktree:
https://linktr.ee/daniela.panetta

Email: daniela.panetta.getresults@gmail.com

CHAPTER 21

My Big Beautiful Bodacious Life

Roxane Archer

"**I**f you were my daughter or sister, I wouldn't do the surgery."

It felt as if all the color suddenly drained from the world. There I was, sitting in the doctor's office, staring at my CT scan — and for a moment, for the first time in my life, I just wanted to call it quits. I was exhausted.

Maybe just giving in is the answer now. Maybe it'll take all the pain away. Maybe it's the easiest thing to do.

But then, instead, a fire lit inside me. It burned in my belly and screamed in my head.

You are a warrior, you are an Archer, you do not give up. What the heck is wrong with you? You've got this, you are strong and have been through too much to let this doctor tell you there is nothing to be done.

After all, what did he know? He knew nothing about me, my strength, my determination. All he knew about me was what the CT scan was telling him. This diagnosis was not my identity; it was not what defined me. I was twenty-eight years old and thought I had it all figured out. I was married and had a great career as a business owner alongside my spouse. We had been traveling the world and truly enjoying life. I spent the summers in my hometown of Invermere, British Columbia, Canada, and the winters in different tropical destinations. Life was great until it wasn't.

Family tragedy had started the previous October, with my dad's second wife finally succumbing to a lifelong disease. Watching my dad say goodbye was incredibly difficult. I had always seen my dad as strong and invincible, the toughest guy I knew, but grief has no boundaries; it breaks even the strongest. Watching him go through the heartbreak of his loss was the first time I had ever really experienced how deeply grief is felt. I wanted to be strong for him like he always was for me, but I didn't know how.

I was pregnant with my first child at the time. I had started reading all the books and planning names, and I remember sharing the news with my family that Christmas. I don't know who was more excited, me or my sister-in-law, who was more like a "real" sister because I had known her since I was eight years old.

On Easter weekend my uncle passed away from a sudden heart attack. I was in my eighth month of pregnancy by then, and a week after his death my water broke. I was hospitalized, put on bed rest, and after several tests and three weeks later, it was determined my baby had a rare condition called Triploidy. She would not survive long outside of me.

My beautiful daughter Hayley Alisha was born at the end of May, a week before her due date, and passed away immediately. It was not the outcome I had dreamed of.

Leaving the hospital empty-handed, going home to an empty nursery, and having to call my family to tell them is still one of my darkest moments. It was heartache like I had never imagined. I blamed myself. In my head I went over all the things I did. I tried to make sense of it, but there was no sense to be made.

A month later, I had started to feel unwell. I was tired all the time, sleeping seventeen hours a day, with spiking high fevers lasting a couple of days at a time. I was experiencing headaches, and occasionally fainting. The doctors kept telling me it was stress.

That so-called stress gave me a big wakeup call on a cold December day when I woke with a high fever yet again, and a yellow tinge in my skin. I immediately went to the hospital. After several days and many tests, I found myself sitting in that doctor's office staring at an image showing a mass the size of an orange growing in my head. If I didn't have the tumor removed, it would surely take my life, and if I did have it removed, the surgery would probably take my life. Apparently, the specialist I was sitting with didn't want a twenty-eight-year-old's death on his surgical resume; he was refusing to operate.

Weeks went by, and I couldn't bring myself to tell my family the news. I remember picking up the phone so many times, but it felt like a hundred pounds in my hand, and I couldn't dial because I didn't know how I was going to get the words out.

I went to bed one night, telling myself *tomorrow is the day I tell them.*

The next morning, before I could call my brother with my news, he called me and asked me to sit down. His wife (my sister-in-law) and their youngest daughter were in a car accident and passed away. The world felt like it had stopped until I realized it was me who had stopped breathing for what seemed like forever. Our family had been through so much already. This was all within a fourteen-month period.

I didn't dare share the bombshell of my own health crisis. There was no way I could say anything. My brother was broken, and his remaining daughter was distraught; so much had been taken away in the blink of an eye. And I was supposed to tell them they could lose me too?

Nope, not happening.

So it was my secret to keep for a while longer. I just couldn't bring myself to tell my dad, having lost his wife, brother, and now his daughter-in-law and second granddaughter. How was I supposed to tell him he could lose his only daughter? I am the youngest of four, with three older brothers. I am the baby of the family. I couldn't bring myself to put more stress on them. It was a hard secret to keep, but I felt in my heart the timing wasn't right. I wanted to protect my family. I wanted to take their pain away.

Four months went by before I finally told them, after I had gotten a second, third, and fourth medical opinion. It was the last specialist who agreed the tumor needed to be removed, and he was up for the challenge. He was so sure of himself that it gave me confidence and hope. A month later I was wheeled into a six-hour surgery. It was a long recovery, but a success.

I realize now we must embrace the pain in all its stages to truly heal, but it took me many years and a lot of personal development to come to that. It also took me going through even more loss to truly know what it means to live a life of gratitude.

My marriage fell apart because you either grow closer through tragedy or you grow apart. Years later I also lost two of my brothers within one year. Their deaths were eleven months apart, and they were both only forty-nine years old.

And then there was the loss of my mom. My relationship with her had been a challenge throughout my entire life, and I believe she suffered from mental health issues and generational trauma. She had not been able to find the strength to overcome her struggles, and instead of walking through the pain towards healing, she held on to her pain like a safety blanket, not realizing it was more harmful than comforting. She was a beautiful person caught in an internal battle of what was real and what wasn't. She had a distorted perspective of reality, which caused mental misery to herself and others around her.

I was her youngest child, and after my brothers moved out I had been left on my own to try to cope with her behavior. She walked through life believing there was an evil plot, everyone was out to get her, and she blamed everyone else for her own actions. She loved me one day and seemed to hate me the next — a trauma that has haunted me most of my life. She was passing her generational trauma on to me like a family legacy.

I had always felt like I was never good enough, and no matter how much I wanted a better life, I was undeserving. I had silenced the inner voice that whispered to me that *I could be great, I could have an amazing life, I could do amazing things, and my life was going to be beautiful.* For many years she silenced my dreams and kept me from truly being my authentic self.

When my mom went missing, I found myself experiencing conflicting emotions. I wondered if she had taken off somewhere, was it planned, did something happen to her, was she hurt? I went over and over in my mind where she could be. She was a missing person for three years until her remains were found, and we were finally able to get some answers and have closure.

Through each of these devastating losses I was forced to look inside for strength. I didn't want to be strong, but I felt like there was no other choice. We can overcome and grow stronger, or we can be a victim and become weaker. As crazy as this sounds, my mom's death was the catalyst that made me truly realize who I was. Going through her belongings and reading letters and journals she had written forced me to learn more about how she thought, which allowed me to forgive her.

Instead of resenting my mom for who she was, and what she did to me, I started loving her for what she did for me. I would not be the loving mother I am, the compassionate friend, have a heart filled with kindness and I would not have the integrity I have, if it wasn't for her trying to break me. Because she was broken, she wanted to transfer her pain on to others. She built me strong trying to tear me down, and in being able to forgive her, I realized who I really was. I felt at peace. I felt aligned. And for the first time in my life, I could say I loved her.

I have chosen to find the gifts within the struggles, the peace within the pain. The universe sends us a message, tests us, and pushes us to our limits to show us who we can be and what we are capable of. Can you imagine a life without any struggles? How would you grow and become better, find your strengths, reach your potential, find your true, authentic self, and be able to help others through relatability if your life was a picture of perfection?

I used to hate it when people said, "Roxane, you are so strong." This drove me crazy. I wasn't strong; sometimes I was barely hanging on. Sometimes I held darkness very close to my heart. I just kept making the choice to not become a victim; I just chose to see blessings; I just chose to always move forward even though sometimes it was strides and sometimes it was baby steps; I just chose not to be defined by grief and loss. After all, it was just the universe testing me, because I was destined to be better. It was never easy, but it was necessary, and with every struggle and every loss, I became better.

No matter how much I wanted to avoid the pain, I learned I cannot hide from it. The process of going through pain helps us grow and become a better version of ourselves. I walked into the eye of the storm, broken, and came out whole, and now I share my experiences to inspire others to have the confidence to face their struggles, tackle their goals, and achieve their happiness. We need to create the conditions for happiness and abundance to occur. How many of us don't allow ourselves to feel good because we are too busy beating ourselves up, and too busy telling ourselves we can't have the life we desire and deserve?

Because I forgave not only my mom, but also myself, I stopped the legacy of generational trauma in my family. My son will be free to dream of greatness. I am excited now to go after all those dreams that whispered to me but were silenced. I always felt like I was meant to make a difference, help others, and be influential, and now I have created the space for these things to happen.

We are not the product of our upbringing or our past. We are the product of what we decide, and we are all just a choice or two away from a great life. Sometimes we need to ask ourselves better questions when we are facing challenges.

Would we rather have a picture-perfect, easy life? Sounds boring to me. I will take messy and chaotic any day. I want to be the old lady the neighbors talk about, sitting on my porch swing, sipping wine, sharing my outrageous stories and my smiles abundantly. I want to be full of life and laughter up to the end because what are we living for if we can't find the blessings even in the darkest times? I want to bring tears to people's eyes when I tell my life story, some tears of empathy but mostly the tears that make you cross your legs because you are laughing so hard. I want to be known for my quirkiness and my weird sense of humor, not my tragedies, though it was those tragedies that made me quirky and gave me a better sense of humor.

Are you going to keep going backwards, reliving your past, and holding on to your safety blanket? Or are you going to light that blanket on fire, shine brightly with your gifts, dream big, and visualize a magnificent life of happiness?

Stop worrying about the past and just create a life of laughter and a future you get excited about. Stop worrying about finding balance; there is no such thing. It's all just organized chaos. The messier the life, the more rewarding it is.

Through loss, my pain has taught me gratitude and to live in the moment, rather than to pack around the past like a safety blanket I just can't let go of. I learned to embrace the good and the bad, I learned nothing will break us if we choose to not let it do so, and tears are okay; they are how we cleanse our soul. I have built a life of abundance by choice. I have an amazing son, a beautiful stepdaughter, and a spouse who makes me laugh and smile every day. They fill my heart with love. I have built a successful career making a difference in people's lives, and I cherish all my family and the time I have with them. I have surrounded myself with amazing people and my small circle of friends are golden.

I am living my big, beautiful, bodacious life, and it is only going to get better because I never stop visualizing the abundance the world has to offer. It is there for us to create whatever we want; we just must believe in ourselves and give ourselves permission to reach for it.

About the Author

Roxane Archer is a mom to a very witty, amazing son and a beautiful, intelligent stepdaughter, and is a spouse to an incredibly handsome man. She is a bit sarcastic, loves sunshine and beaches, and lovingly suffers through her spouse's addiction to loud music, shoes, and Halloween masks. She is a house-plant killer and dark chocolate lover. She is incredibly loyal to those around her, and always puts her family before anything else. She is the youngest of four and had three older brothers who taught her many great qualities, but mostly survival skills, as they lovingly tormented her like typical older brothers do.

Roxane is a wealth management entrepreneur and financial educator who inspires and empowers others to overcome challenges and create their dreams. She works online from her home in British Columbia, Canada, and before owning her own agency in the financial services industry, she had an eclectic background of jobs. She cut down trees for Christmas tree farms, was a lifeguard, a business owner in the stock trading industry taking companies public on the NASDAQ stock exchange, and she also worked for many years in the healthcare industry (cardiology). Her volunteer work has included helping bring smiles to children's faces through the Make a Wish® Foundation, as well as volunteering on school field trips and participating on parent association committees with the schools.

Roxane's mission is to help people achieve their life goals through financial stability and education, and to help change their financial legacy. She knows how unpredictable life is and that preparation for the unknown is one of the best gifts we can give our loved ones. She is also passionate about helping others heal through their own traumas and loss by sharing her experiences, and she hopes her story can help others. Roxane believes our smile is our superpower, and that the world needs more smiles and kindness in it.

Connect with Roxane to find out more about how she helps her clients and inspires others through her story.

Facebook:
https://www.facebook.com/roxane.archer.5

Instagram:
https://www.instagram.com/roxanearcher/

LinkedIn:
https://www.linkedin.com/in/roxane-archer-b10719a3/

Email: roxanearcher@gmail.com

Absolute Vision

Closing words from Jo Pronger Faulkner

I am thrilled to bring you this second collaboration in the *Absolute* series, and to connect you with this team of incredible men and women from around the world. Despite the struggles and difficult decisions they faced in their journeys, each of these authors have reframed their life's experiences to create lessons of wisdom and inner strength from which we can all gain clarity.

Whenever we feel stuck, unhappy, unfulfilled, or as though we are drifting through life, it's not usually because of a lack of motivation; the more common reason is a lack of vision, or one that is flat and needs a little CPR. While reflecting upon the life vision we had may seem like a light-hearted, uplifting exercise, the reality is revisiting our goals and dreams and taking an honest, close-up look at where we are now, compared to where we thought we'd be, can feel like a gut-punch if we believe we haven't "made it" yet.

The good news is our story isn't over until we take our last breath, and in the meantime we get to pick up a pen, turn to a fresh page, and script our "vision revival scene" however we want it to play out.

I hope within these pages you have found yourself realizing your imagination isn't just child's play, dreaming isn't a waste of time, and wanting something more — something bigger, something better — is still possible, no matter what circumstances you've been through.

Nervous butterflies might try to chase away your dreams, or fear and grief might try to stop you in your tracks, but going after what you really want requires letting go of what you don't. The truth is, only YOU can decide what's right for you, what greatest vision you want to fulfill, and what a big, bodacious, extraordinary life feels like to you.

Made in the USA
Middletown, DE
12 December 2022